BATMAN ™

BATMAN™

THE OFFICIAL BOOK OF THE MOVIE

JOHN MARRIOTT

MALLARD
PRESS

Acknowledgements
The Publishers gratefully acknowledge the invaluable assistance of Gordon
Arnell, Tricia Fisher and Judy Britten of the *Batman* publicity office;
Phyllis Hume of DC Comics Inc., Bud Rosenthal of Warner Bros.; and
Keith Isaac of Licensing Corporation of America (Europe) Limited.

Photographic acknowledgements
Cover photograph: Herb Ritts/Warner Bros.
All other photographs: Murray Close/Warner Bros.; Keith Hamshere/
Warner Bros.; Douglas Luke/Warner Bros.

Designed by Kit Johnson and Ran Barnes.

Cover photographs
Front: Batman (Michael Keaton)
Back (clockwise from the top): Bruce Wayne (Michael Keaton); The Joker
(Jack Nicholson); Alicia Hunt (Jerry Hall); The Batmobile; Carl Grissom
(Jack Palance); Vicki Vale (Kim Basinger).

An Imprint of BDD Promotional Book Company, Inc.
666 Fifth Avenue
New York, N.Y. 10103

First published in the United States of America in 1989 by
The Mallard Press
By arrangement with The Hamlyn Publishing Group Ltd, a division of
The Octopus Publishing Group, Michelin House, 81 Fulham Road,
London SW3 6RB
ISBN 0-792-45125-2

CONTENTS

FOREWORD

Batman is very extreme and I love extreme characters. A man who dresses up as a bat and his arch rival who is transformed into a clown are very popular images and one of the reasons why Batman remains so popular.

Batman is not a super-hero, he's not a guy from another planet. So I like to take a straightforward approach and just present it.

Making movies of this size and complexity is very much a team effort, in our case involving a squad of almost six hundred, and in the following pages you will meet some of the key people.

Whether you know Batman from books, the comics, television or even if you don't know him at all, I think what you will have is a very interesting, surprising action story with a bunch of weird characters running around.

What more could you want?

TIM BURTON

FROM FEAR TO FROLICS

THE STORY OF BATMAN

Beetlejuice director Tim Burton has made his own version of Batman for the big screen. Commissioned by Warner Bros., and a product of his own imagination, it owes more to the early comics than the television series but will find no difficulty in attracting fans of both.

KANE'S CREATION

Biff! Pow! Holy Crimewave! The oddball exclamations which peppered the much-loved TV series of Batman denote an out-to-lunch attitude and lunatic wit with which several generations of viewers are now familiar. In each and every episode the firm-jawed Batman and his gee-whizz companion Robin would knock out, then lock up, assorted weirdo villains in a manner which parodied the superhero stance. Maximum merriment was created by playing straight, with poker faces proving the best weapon for firing off fun lines and loopy dialogue.

And yet Batman was not always so. The comic-strip camp of the television adventures must have struck *Detective Comics* (DC) readers as completely alien. They had been weaned on a superhero who was more sinister street vigilante than gaudy joker, a threatening presence who was more likely to cause his enemies to panic than to laugh.

Until 1937, most comic books were stuffed with predictable re-runs of newspaper cartoon strips. It was in this year that DC brightened up a dull market by introducing the detective figure as central to all their comic-book action. Though at once successful, these new comics were not shot through with superhero antics until the following year, when *Action Comics* (a spin-off from *Detective Comics*) provided a star platform for Superman.

Readership soared and America was quickly gripped by superhero fever. Healthy, clean-cut symbols of the American Dream, they usually combined great strength with interesting clothes, a description which also applies to Batman himself.

Initially referred to as *the* Batman, this eerie, nocturnal creature was the next big superhero after Superman. It was only when, later on, Batman stepped out of the shadows to play a full part in public life that he was more warmly referred to as just plain Batman.

Aside from a secret identity, a mission to fight crime and a penchant for fancy dress, the two heroes were markedly different. Unlike the garish attire of Superman, the original Batman sported a dark outfit, including a cape whose cut resembled a pair of bat wings which were a fitting expression of his nocturnal status. Moreover, unlike Superman, he was not possessed of any super powers. He relied simply on physical prowess, an agile mind and an ability to frighten lawbreakers into next week to score points for virtue.

Secret identities were not a product of comic book invention. In the writings of Baroness Orczy, Sir Percy Blakeney was revealed as The Scarlet Pimpernel, while in Johnston McCulley's stories, El Zorro's true identity was that of a wealthy young poet, Don Diego Vega. Thus the Batman/Bruce Wayne double act was only tapping into an established literary tradition.

Bob Kane, Batman's creator, openly acknowledges his debt to Douglas Fairbanks Sr., who was the first actor to play Zorro on the big screen. It was Zorro's fearless physical adventures which caused Kane to conceive his hero as an 'acro-Batman'.

Kane also gives credit to The Shadow, a cloaked vigilante who used to sneak through the city by night. Yet aside from big cloak and angled hat, The Shadow dressed like any other man. Fixing his imagination again onto outside sources, Kane took Batman's costume from both Superman himself and from the

*The easy poise and comfortable smile of Batman creator Bob Kane (seen here on the set of **Batman**) do not readily suggest the creepy nocturnal avenger of the early comics. The Joker's malicious glee never deters Batman from swooping from the skies to catch criminals off guard.*

villain in a 1926 movie called *The Bat*. By employing a villain's bat costume to cloak a hero, Kane added a twist to the expected appearance of a righteous avenger and so added character depth. Kane also points to the similarity between the name Bruce Wayne and his own name, admitting that in drawing Batman he was living out his own teenage fantasies. He rightly assumed that Batman would give readers a vicarious thrill. Kane has, however, hinted elsewhere that Bruce was taken from Robert the Bruce, the macho Scots king, while Wayne was inspried by 'Mad' Anthony Wayne, hero of the Revolutionary War.

It would have been unthinkable for the TV Batman to kill a criminal himself, since he always felt duty-bound to operate within the law and so turn up at Gotham City police HQ like a good boy scout, tweaking his prey by the ear. And yet in the early comic book days, Batman was much more the vigilante and less the goody-two-shoes. In *'The Case of the Chemical Syndicate'* (1939), the police actively hunt down Batman, since they deeply resent his treading on their turf. Back then, Batman, like other

Lit by a full moon, the early Batman slinks through the night to fight The Monk (1939), before confronting the noisy mockery of The Joker two years later. By the time Batman encounters the killer clown in the early Fifties, an element of fun has pierced the darkness.

cartoon superheroes, flouted the law and dispatched a criminal if he felt he deserved it. Whereas the TV crusader would knock an enemy on the head with a couple of quick biffs and wait for the bumbling flatfoots to arrive, Batman spouting heroic truisms all the while, the early *Detective Comics* vigilante would act as pursuer, prosecution and jury and so clean up the streets in five minutes flat. This also explains the need for a masked identity, as much to avoid the police as the hoods themselves.

Batman entered the public arena more and more, especially after the appearance of Robin, whose full-frontal blast of red, green and yellow presumably handicapped his boss from sliding through the shadows. Inspired in both name and costume by Robin Hood, the Boy Wonder was added by Kane, one year after the emergence of Batman, as a character who could win over young readers. Kane here admits too that Robin was as much the embodiment of his boyhood fantasies as Batman had been of his teen dreams. Unlike children who had accompanied adult heroes in literature (and also in comic strips like 'Dickie Dare' and 'Terry and the

Pirates'), Robin did not exist to upstage Batman but to assist him in his gutsy pursuit of evil.

ENTER FRIENDS AND FOES

To lend credibility to Robin's partnership with Batman, Robin was introduced in 1940 as a circus acrobat whose dare-devil feats in the big tent would make him a natural companion to his mentor. With Robin's parents already dead (they had been killed), Batman was conveniently at hand to 'adopt' the young man. The successful twinning of man and boy avengers led to many comic book copies: The Green Arrow and Speedy, The Shield and Dusty, Captain America and Bucky were but a few of the successful characters ushered in by the birth of Robin.

Modern-day commentators on Batman, especially those who indulge in two cents analysis, have insisted that homosexuality must have been the bond between a grown man and his boy charge living under the same roof. Jules Feiffer, the cartoonist, insisted

at the time when Batman the TV series was first a hit, that the two chaps were indeed homosexuals. William Dozier, executive producer of the show, popped up regularly on TV to rebuff such accusations, while simultaneously admitting that the inclusion of Aunt Harriet (who first appeared in the DC strip in 1964) was a ploy 'to keep them from looking like homosexuals. We put a woman in the house to balance the act.'

Yet homosexuality was hardly part of Bob Kane's original plan. Whereas other heroes thought themselves lucky if one girlfriend were drawn in to share the story, Batman must have loved Kane for providing him with a real galaxy. Conceiving Bat-

man's alter ego, millionaire Bruce Wayne, as a playboy, Kane first linked his creation to Julie Madison (his fiancee for a while), before fixing him up with Linda Page, a society girl who gave up glitz and glamour for nursing so that she also could truly serve mankind.

Another girlfriend appeared in the form of photo-journalist Vicki Vale. A little too similar in essence to Superman's girlfriend Lois Lane, Vicki spent more time trying to come up with Batman's identity than she did in the arms of Bruce Wayne. The opportunities here for amusing irony were usually taken.

The Batwoman, like Robin, a former circus whizz, appeared also at this time and proceeded to fight Vicki for Bruce's attentions. Kane, in order to concentrate Batman on his mission, was careful to remove any lady who really threatened to hook him.

With the rapid success of the comic-book Batman, it proved impossible for Kane to do all the artwork himself. Batman's appearance in *Detective Comics*, *World's Finest Comics*, *Batman*, as well as a newspaper cartoon which began in 1943, meant that

FROM FEAR TO FROLICS

11

Jerry Robinson, Win Mortimer, Jim Mooney, Carmine Infantino, Dick Sprang and Mort Meskin rallied to the call, although Kane always insisted that his own by-line appear.

It was not Kane who wrote the stories, though he would often conceive the characters in them. The main writer was a man by the name of Bill Finger whose stories often featured huge working versions of commonplace objects: king-size sewing machines really clicked and sewed, huge record players gave off the sound of music, while killer tubes of paint were packed with the real stuff.

Finger provided a battery of gadgets which could fox Batman's sworn enemies, of whom surely The Joker, a practical joker propelled by malice, is still the most memorable. Bill Finger speaks affectionately of the origins of the character.

Kane called Finger with an idea for a killer who looked like a clown. When Bill saw Bob's sketch, he thought the Joker looked more amusing than sinister. Finger happened to have a series of stills from the movie version of Victor Hugo's *The Man Who Laughs*, the 1928 film in which Conrad Veidt had played lead. The story centres on Gwynplaine, an English nobleman who was kidnapped as a child and converted into a circus freak through having a fiendish grin carved onto his face. The stills of Veidt with appropriately disquieting make-up assisted Finger in producing the perfect Joker.

The success of The Joker soon led to a parade of quirky characters whose purpose was to confront Batman. The Penguin, the Riddler (who only popped up in two stories in the 1940s but was revived as a superstar in the TV series), Catwoman (who began life as a jewel thief called the Cat), the Scarecrow (who quickly vanished only to reappear later), Tweedledum and Tweedledee, Punch and Judy and Two-Face. This latter enemy was an extremely versatile creation and even spawned two fake Two-Faces.

BATMAN ON SCREEN

Aside from appearing on radio alongside Superman, Batman and Robin twice hit the big screen. *Batman* was a movie serial by Columbia Pictures which was a major break for two relative unknowns, Lewis Wilson (Batman) and Douglas Croft (Robin). The only other character to leap from comic book to movie set was Alfred, the butler, while newcomer Linda was introduced as Batman's girlfriend. But many were disappointed at the hero's almost baggy costume and

1973

1988

Having suffered bouts of sci-fi silliness,
Batman has more recently returned as the
scary figure of old. Sprung like a panther
with lantern jaw to the fore (1973),
he is fitting match for
The Joker who drips evil (1988).

felt that the points on his cowl bore too close a resemblance to the devil's horns. It is probable that the new thin Arthur, with English moustache, prompted the redrawing of him in the comic books. Efficient though the avenging twosome was, both were upstaged by the great character actor J. Carroll Nash who played Japanese nasty, Dr Daka. In 1943, anti-Japanese sentiment seemed justified and barely caused a flutter. Yet the subtext of the serial, which congratulated the interment of Nisei by the American government on the basis that all Japanese were the devil on earth, made many squirm in the Sixties when the serial was bolted together as a single feature and thus re-released.

In 1948 Columbia made a second foray into the same territory, with a further serial *Batman and Robin*, in which Robert Lowery and John Duncan fought off a villain called the Wizard and came to terms with lots of sci-fi gadgetry. Alfred was no longer around to serve tea. Worthy though it was, this effort still could not recreate the imaginative universe of the comic books.

In the comics, meanwhile, Batman had joined Superman on a number of adventures before being spun off into space in the late Fifties to enter the realm of science fiction. Never a sci-fi character like Superman, Batman lost credibility through these bouts of silliness. In 1964, realism crept in again through the back door. A few years later, Robin went to college (!) and Batman bought a penthouse in Gotham City from which he ran the VIP (Victims Incorporated Program). The comic-strip circle was neatly completed by the immediate reappearance of *the* Batman, the frightening avenger of the dark.

It was the smash-hit TV series which created an imaginative riot on screen which some believe exceeded the fantasy of the comic book adventures. A planet away from the sinister threats and tough-guy behaviour of the DC Batman, the series chucked out malice and brought in camp. Executive producer William Dozier explains:
'I had the simple idea of overdoing it, of making it so square and so serious that adults would find it amusing. I knew kids would go for the derring-do, the adventure, but the trick would be to find adults who would either watch it with their kids or, to hell with

the kids, and watch it anyway.' According to Dozier, Adam West as Batman was quick to grasp that 'it had to be played as though we were dropping a bomb on Hiroshima, with that kind of deadly seriousness.'

Teaming up with Burt Ward as Robin, West fronted a show which was not only unique in tone but also in its use of brand new special effects. It captured an audience of all age groups and social classes. Dozier's dream had come true.

The high cost of producing the show (particularly in the realm of special effects) played a large part in its final demise but cleared a path for a cartoon series of Batman which successfully ran on Saturday morning television in the US in the late Sixties. In 1977, another cartoon series was made, on this occasion bringing back West and Ward as voices, while both reappeared in two live action specials in 1979 whose aim was to resurrect the Batman series. Both specials, unfortunately, announced loudly too

'The film will be **the** *highlight of Batman's*
long career. The Topper of the whole
mystique.'
Bob Kane, creator of Batman.

that they had been made on video tape for three dollars and a piece of string. West has continued to lend his voice to the character of Batman in the 'Super Friends' cartoon series.

Noting that a mint copy of the first issue of *Detective Comics*, which sold in May 1939 for 10 cents, is now worth at least $20,000, Bob Kane, who is also production consultant on the movie, remembers ironically: 'My ex-wife threw out all my collection. I don't mind the divorce, but I only wish I had the comic books! When my stockbroker calls me and says "Shall I buy any more stock?" I say, "No, Charlie – buy comic books!"'

In 1939 the World's Fair took place at Flushing Meadows, New York. Batman sketches were among the artifacts which were buried in a time capsule which is due to be opened in the year 2000.

It is the terrific enthusiasm for and loyalty to the Batman character which Warner Bros. hope to tap for the new movie. Following Tim Burton's intention to return Batman to his more solemn role as a sinister street vigilante, the story will tweak the heartstrings of DC fans but may at first put off the die-hards who glued themselves to the weekly world of TV camp. Both groups will be satisfied, since the edge-of-the-seat thrills, which are provided by a serious man-with-a-mission, are also laced with humour.

BURTON BEETLEJUICE AND BATMAN

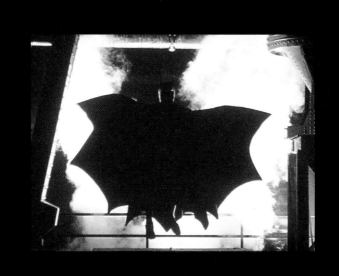

As director of the film, Tim Burton is an inspired choice. Even when collaborating on the first treatment, he was determined to 'take it back to a darker vision, a dark melodrama, but with the added benefit of absurd humour.' He was also keen to remove the humour from the campy buffoonery of the television series, and to 'play it with a straight face which would leave room for laughs.'

Although admitting that his Batman is closest in spirit, if not in detail, to the earliest DC version, Burton adds that he also wants to give the audience 'a collective history' of the character which includes everything the director has loved about the image of Batman over the years. He argues that a substantial image is often flexible enough to be molded in different ways. He himself cut his teeth as a youngster on the TV series, so by way of preparation, he has had to delve into the comic books which, he points out, went through several changes over the years:

'Batman began as a dark detective before he was later given all kinds of gadgetry to help fight crime. He finally ended up as a camp figure who took off on adventures which never even occurred at night. Unlike Superman, who has remained pretty much true to himself, Batman has changed quite a bit.' Tim professes a preference for 'extreme characters who are, however, strongly based on reality.'

Part of Batman's realism is that he has what the director calls a 'contemporary sensibility', and is 'at heart a vigilante. I have a lot of trouble dealing with vigilante themes. The only way I could create a *Death Wish*-type situation was by balancing Batman's crime-stopping antics with absurd humour. The humour is very important to me'.

Above: *Tim Burton's intention was always to return Batman to his role as a sinister street vigilante who caused both fear and respect. The appearance of Batman on the streets of Gotham City is enough to shake Jack Napier.*

Right: *Tim Burton established his penchant for freewheeling anarchy and quirky humour in both* **Beetlejuice** *and* **Pee-Wee's Big Adventure.** *Both elements are present in his version of Batman where an aura of malice is always balanced by a sense of fun.*

An unavoidable product of Movieland, Tim was born in Burbank, and started out as a Disney animator, and before becoming a designer at the Disney studio. Before that, in 1972, as a callow 14-year-old, he had designed an anti-litter poster in 1972 which adorned all the Burbank Basin garbage trucks.

Burton went to Cal Arts from which he was to graduate, and he now believes he learned a lot about directing back then: 'Animation was a much better training for me than a regular film school – you get to do it all yourself.' One of his earliest childhood fantasies had been to be 'one of those guys in a monster costume who wrecks a miniature Tokyo. Since I couldn't be Godzilla, I decided to be an animator.' Fortunately, Disney appreciated that his talent was not for cute animals and let him do his own thing.

Below and left: *Kim Basinger talks affectionately about how she and Tim understood each other so well that they used the shorthand language of close friends. Tim not only had to direct Kim, but also many complicated special effects sequences. Here the Batmobile is seen torching the Axis Chemical Factory and so reducing it to ruins.*

THE BIG SCREEN

He was finally allowed to give vent to his sense of anarchy on the big screen with *Pee-Wee's Big Adventure*. Pee-Wee Herman is the gangly oddball who, with pancake make-up and loud suit, embarks on a crazy adventure which gives plenty of scope for his surreal and quirky view of the universe. One senses that this is shared by Burton himself.

Tim really became big-time with *Beetlejuice*, which blasted his fruitcake imagination across the movie screens of the world and earned $100 million to boot. With Michael Keaton as the undead corpse who switches from the unsettling world of ghosts to the comfy suburban home of a married couple, it was propelled by a cartoon innocence which is also at the root of Burton's own personality. The director is characteristically modest about the appeal of *Beetlejuice*: 'It has its hits and misses, but I don't mind. When it works, it's fun. When it doesn't, at least I tried something.'

This reward of independence led Tim to direct two shorts which gave ample proof of his interest in the absurd as well as his free-wheeling sense of fun.

Vincent concerned a young boy who obsessively hero-worships Vincent Price, while *Franken Weenie* was dominated by another strange youngster who jump-started his dog by pumping him full of mega-volts.

As Burton speaks of his intention to 'balance the crime-stopping antics with absurd humour', Batman himself listens with due care and attention.

Burton is possessed of a wild imagination and cartoon innocence which fire all his pictures. During a moment of concentration on the set of 'Batman' he manages to resemble both a little boy lost and an adult in control.

When describing his film, Burton spoke of his intention to 'play it with a straight face which would leave room for laughs'. He can't resist the odd grin himself, though.

TIM BURTON

Considered by Warner Bros. to be a with-it director who will wow the kids, Tim Burton has a cartoon innocence which is unsurprising in an ex-Disney animator. A director who brings a vision to all his work, he has also included everything he ever liked about Batman or, in Tim's own words, 'a collective history' of the character. A camera is always turning inside Tim's head.

Having only just turned 30 during the filming of Batman, Burton is very young — and very proud — to be making a film which celebrates the 50th birthday of Batman.

Mark Canton, President of Worldwide Motion Picture Production has spent a lot of time on the set at Pinewood Studios near London, where filming took place, and believes this demonstrates Warners' hands-on attitude towards their pictures. He calls it his favourite project: 'When I first joined Warners nine years ago, I became very involved in the development of Batman,' he says. In his position as head of production, he was able to make the film happen, and was happy to work with Jon Peters and Peter Guber whom he describes as 'two of the great producers'. It was Tim Burton, he says, who 'pointed us in a direction with which we were all happy. He sees it as a hard-edged adventure whose sense of stylish humour is absurd rather than corny. He also likes the way that the Batmobile and the Batwing have become characters in themselves.'

Right: *An artist's impression of the brooding skyline of Gotham City by night is a fitting metaphor for the violent crime which grips it by day.*

Below: *The back lot at Pinewood was used to build Gotham City Centre. The main street is Broad Avenue, which, looking towards the abandoned Cathedral is dominated on screen by a geometric savagery which seems to scorn its citizens.*

Below right: *The Cathedral, which dwarfs every other brutal chunk of architecture, now plays host to a police squad which pursues Batman and The Joker in the final sequence.*

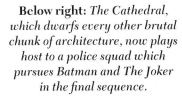

GUBER-PETERS BATMAN PRODUCERS

It took more than a decade of hard work and perseverance to bring Batman to the big screen. The ten-year struggle began in 1979 when executive producers Ben Melniker and Michael Uslan approached DC Comics to obtain the film rights and brought them to Jon Peters and Peter Guber, co-founders of the successful Guber-Peters production company.

Well-known for a string of hits, including *Missing* (1982), *Flashdance* (1983), *A Star Is Born* (1976), *The Witches of Eastwick* (1987), *The Color Purple* (1985), *Gorillas in the Mist* (1988) and the 1989 Academy Award-winner *Rainman*, Guber-Peters has established a firm reputation for producing quality, innovative films. The producers immediately recognized the potential of a screen version of the legendary hero and brought it to Warner Bros., where they have a long-term production relationship. Their version of a Batman feature film was enthusiastically endorsed by top Warner Bros. management.

Several writers and directors worked on the project over the years, before Jon Peters and Peter Guber finally took the reins and the film became a reality. In 1988, they brought in Tim Burton to guide the project and Sam Hamm to pen the script. Working with Burton and Hamm, Peters and Guber were closely involved with the script and casting and they arranged for the film to be made at Pinewood Studios in London. 'The struggle was well worth it,' Peters says. 'We were able to work with some of the best names in the business on this project and the end result reflects the contributions of this enormous pool of talent.'

British co-producer Chris Kenny sees Batman giving a much-needed shot in the arm to the British Film Industry: 'I just hope that the film is a success and that Warner Bros. want to make more. It could be the start of another series of big pictures to be made in this country.'

BATMAN IN ACTION

Below left and right (main picture): *The bold newspaper headline lets us know that we are back in a world where Batman is a sinister avenger. Bruce Wayne's obsessive mission to provide justice-for-all was a direct result of a boyhood trauma, caused by the brutal slaying of his parents at the hands of street thugs.*
Right (inset): *Young Bruce with his wealthy parents who are shortly afterwards cut down in a dingy back street.*

Gotham City on television was about as threatening as candy floss. The scene in Tim Burton's movie is very different, as darker forces constantly strive to squeeze the life out of Gotham City.

Right from the outset, Batman, although constantly on the side of the law, displays an unsettling combination of decency and darkness. He now resembles the sinister figure of the night familiar to fans of the first DC Comics. Eddie and Nick are two punks. Having terrified the wits out of a couple and their young son, they take a well-earned rest on the roof of a tenemant building. As the night creeps in, the 'winged avenger' appears on the roof to dish out punishment. Batman then slams Eddie up against a chimney stack and ensnares Nick in a tangle of wires before dangling him over the roof. Batman announces; 'Tell all your friends, I am the night.'

Above: *Merging completely with the night one minute, and stepping from the shadows the next, Batman has the ability to petrify even Jack Napier.*

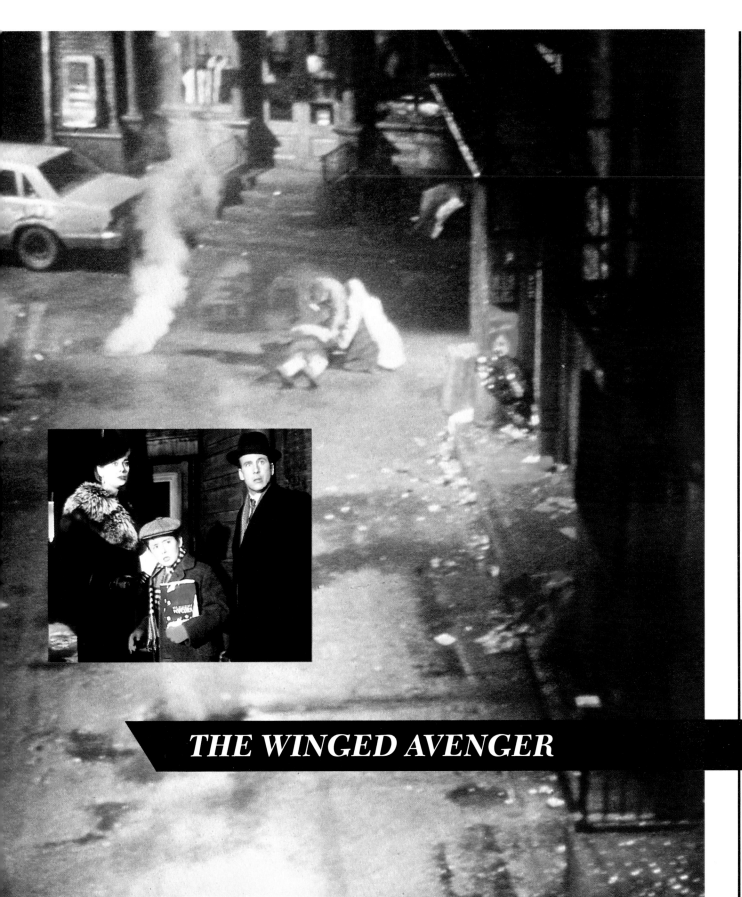

THE WINGED AVENGER

Left: *Commissioner Gordon is flanked by two cops as he contemplates the shoot-out at the Axis Chemical Factory.*

Left: *To distract the police, and give himself time, Jack Napier floods the works with green toxic poison.*

Left: *His cheek pierced, ironically, by one of his own bullets, Jack Napier is now clinging to the catwalk like a scared rabbit.*

HOW JACK BECOMES THE JOKER

Batman's strength seems to be evenly matched by gangster Jack Napier, chief sidekick to bossman Carl Grissom. Napier, played with villainous charm by Jack Nicholson, is a well-dressed thug, whose vanity is as great as his brute force and whose good looks will later vanish to be transformed into The Joker. The first major action sequence of the film concerns Grissom and Napier. Worried that he'll be tied in with dodgy deeds at the Axis Chemical Factory, Grissom sends Jack with a pair of gorillas to do the office over. While one of the hoods aims a blowtorch at the office safe, the others open the filing cabinets.

Hearing sirens outside, they quickly scamper onto a labyrinth of ladders and catwalks which are two stories above the refinery floor. With police bullets puncturing pipes which emit ghastly, multi-coloured vapours Napier jumps to the floor and throws

Left and below: *After foolishly trying to escape the clutches of Batman, Jack Napier takes a plunge into a vat of bubbling toxic waste which will remove his old identity, but provide him with a new one. From this moment on, The Joker will stalk the city.*

switches in order to create a diversion. Colossal machines heave into motion and vast overhead chemical tanks spew out their unpleasant contents into the basins below.

As ever, Batman emerges silently from the shadows, glides easily into action, and leaves a hood dangling 30 feet (9 metres) above the factory floor. He then homes in on Napier. The villain takes an axe to vats marked with the skull-and-crossbones which begin to release a torrent of green poison. The cops retreat in panic, but are not quick enought to avoid the acid fumes.

Almost sucked to freedom by way of the waste disposal chute, Napier finds himself in a Batman-style wrestling hold. He is only released when a hood points a gun at the head of Commissioner Gordon, forcing Batman to let go of his prey.

Napier turns on Batman and shoots him from point blank range. Batman swings his steel gauntlet, the bullet ricochets off it and pierces Napier through the cheek. Staggering in pain, he topples over the walkway, but succeeds in clutching onto the edge. Batman, again proving himself as human as he is vengeful, makes a grab for the murderer, but he loses his grip and Napier slips down into a cauldron of bubbling, toxic waste.

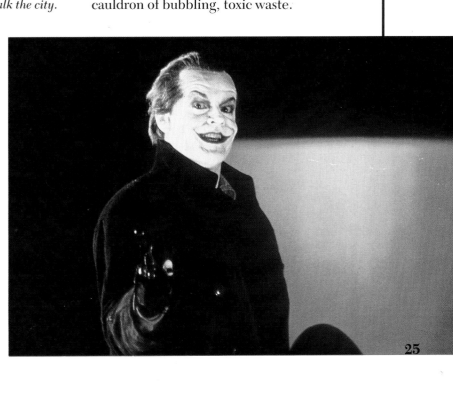

The Joker has arrived at the Flugelheim Museum for a candlelit encounter with Vicki Vale. To minimise interference, Gotham City's best-dressed criminal gasses both art lovers and waiters and next creates a romantic mood with some instant music from his ghetto blaster. Fortunately Batman is at hand to whisk Vicki to safety in the Batmobile.

With Batman himself avoiding the police and vanishing into the night. Napier escapes to the surgery of a seedy backstreet doctor who has striven to salvage something of Jack's face. As the two-cents doctor peels back the bandage, his expression turns to one of horror at the sight of his own handiwork. Napier, demanding a mirror, is no less pleased at the transformation, and staggers off into the night.

Napier now been transformed into The Joker and as such is a committed enemy of all things civilized. He enters The Flugelheim Museum, Gotham City's sole sign of culture and finer feelings, and wreaks havoc. Despite the gallery's brutal exterior, its fern-filled tea room helps the art patrons and tourists forget that their lives have been invaded by a mad grin.

This time, the grin is preceded by choking purple fumes which billow from the air-vent, causing mayhem. With artsy beret balancing at just the right angle, The Joker bursts into the room, his ugly gang in tow. A high-octane ghetto-blaster and cans of aerosol invade a quiet space which is normally super-civil-

MAYHEM AT THE MUSEUM

ized. Those paintings which are not now enhanced by the addition of a broad grin, are clouded out with spray paint.

Only Vicki Vale, the enterprising photo-journalist, played by Kim Basinger, wears a gas-mask supplied in advance by The Joker; she remains conscious, though terrified. Before The Joker has time to trick her with his special flower, Batman smashes through a sky-light and whisks Vicki away from the Flugelheim Museum, on a specially strengthened wire fired from his speargun.

THE BATCAVE

Batman, with Vicki in tow, escapes The Flugelheim and he summons The Batmobile. With a simple voice command, the steel plates retract, the engines roar to life and the obedient vehicle goes to collect its driver, signalling dutifully at the crossroads. Even Batman's car bows to the law. He commands it to stop and Batman and Vicki are soon screeching off at high speed.

They drive out of Gotham City and eventually arrive at a cliff wall. However, it proves to be a mirror projection which acts as a handy entrance to the Batcave.

As befits the sinister timelessness of

The Batcave, although at first seeming like a hollow which time forgot, is paradoxically packed with state-of-the-art gadgetry. Banks of screens and switches assist Bruce Wayne in his deeper thinking and allow him to watch The Joker's every move. Batman brings a bewildered Vicki Vale here after saving her from The Joker's clutches at the Flugelheim Museum.

Batman himself, the cave is a dank world of perpetual night on which the passage of time seems to have made no impact. Avoiding stalactites, which drop from the ceiling, Batman and Vicki make their way through a maze of cramped, craggy passageways which seem to disappear into an indeterminate void.

And then we are suddenly jump-started into the present. A state-of-the-art crime lab makes a perfect partner for an up-to-date tool shop, both of which nestle under vast banks of blinking computers. Although justice-for-all is not dependent on high-tech novelties, Batman shows good common sense in picking up a handful along the way to help the cause.

The unseen screaming bats overhead suggest the dark terror which Batman can inspire in his enemies, while the wounded bat which he keeps in a cage reveals his unwavering humanity.

Batman decides he must destroy The Joker's toxic operation, so he sends along his car to the Axis Chemical factory. Roaring down the street, shooting clouds from multiple exhausts, the Batmobile powers its way through the company gates before coming to a halt in front of the main doors. As the guards' bullets bounce off the bodywork, rockets are released, which smash through the tough steel doors.

The Goons' machine-gun attack, as expected, cannot penetrate the Batmobile, which again shields itself with its steel armour, hunkering down like a metal butterfly. Its tightly packed cache of lethal plastic explosives wipes out the poisons plant. Since the car is bomb-proof, the Batmobile once more growls into life and slides powerfully out of the wreckage summoned by its master. Like a well-trained cat which has just got rid of a houseful of pesky mice, the Batmobile on its return receives an affectionate pat on the fender from its owner.

AXIS CHEMICAL UNDER FIRE

An early attempt of Batman to rub out The Joker does not quite work. With the aid of the Batmobile, Batman turns the Axis Chemical Factory into a dazzling ball of flames. The Goons' paltry gunfire simply bounces off the world's finest car, but The Joker has again skipped clear by means of his helicopter from which he now scorns Batman through a megaphone.

Still, The Joker has managed to escape the blast, and proceeds to take a leading role in Gotham City's 200th Anniversary celebrations. Nervy pedestrians witness a procession of floats to which are attached giant balloons, on each one of which is painted a ghoulish face with stretched grin. The Joker, meanwhile, plans to avoid death by donning a gas-mask, while filling his balloons with a noxious poison that will leave the citizens with a killer smile.

Batman has by now garaged the Batmobile, and brought out the Batwing, his high-powered flying machine. Such are its aerodynamics that it can slice through the night at high speed. With its familiar bat wings, it resembles a mechanical version of its master. Batman looks down on scenes of mayhem.

In a last-ditch attempt to save the good people of Gotham City, Batman uses the Batwing to cut through the ropes which tether the balloons, and so prevent the bystanders from being gassed to death.

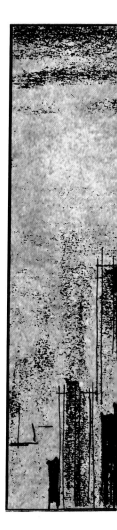

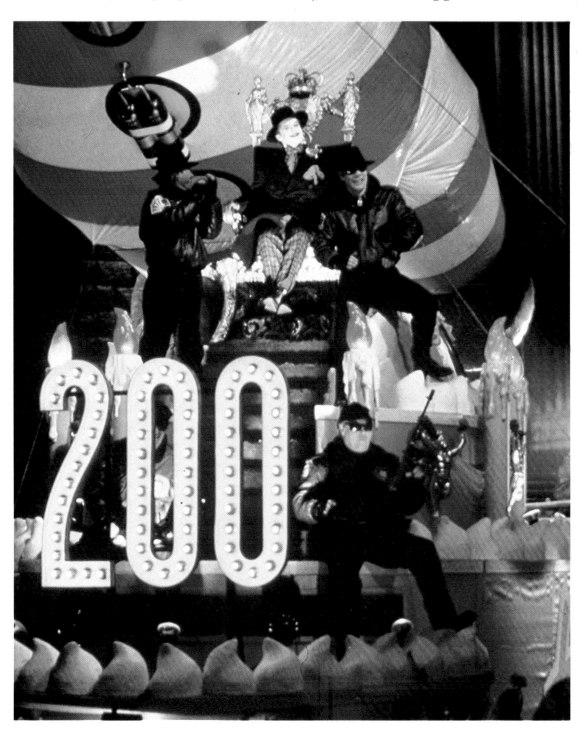

3.

Spoiling The Joker's attempt to wipe out the population with poison-gas balloons, the Batwing pulls them clear of Gotham City just before they are meant to explode.

THE JOKER ON PARADE

JOKER REACTS TO THE
OVERHEAD BATWING —
DISMOUNTS FROM THE FLOAT,
¢ MY BALLOONS→!

PROCESSION SEQ. BATBOARDS

BATMAN SCENE 213 BD.# 1

TB/MW I/XI. 88 PINEWOOD

2.

Scarcely believing that he has again been thwarted by Batman, The Joker removes his gas mask as he steps down from the float.

BATWING PULLS OUT OF A
VERTICAL DIVE & LEVELS AT
ABOUT 30 FEET EXITS.
(THIS SHOULD BRING HIM BELOW THE BALLOONS)

PROCESSION SEQ. BATBOARDS

BATMAN SCENE 207 BD.# 1

TB/MW I/XI. 88 PINEWOOD

1.

In an attempt to foil The Joker's plans, the Batwing pulls out of a vertical dive and levels off to bring it between the float and the balloons.

THE FINAL CONFRONTATION

Left: *One shot from The Joker's amazingly long pistol has been sufficient to send the Batwing crashing onto the cathedral steps. With only rattled nerves and torn cape, Batman is poised to follow The Joker into the Cathedral.*

Above: *The Joker, who has taken Vicki Vale hostage, now graces the Cathedral belfry as he swings Vicki through a dance routine before his planned escape.*

Batman readies his craft for the final assault on his enemy. An arsenal is let loose from the air but The Joker, leaping manically as is his way, succeeds in avoiding it all. With one blast from his long gun, the Joker fills the Batwing's cockpit with smoke, causing the engines to cut out. Dancing a victory jig, he watches the Batwing belly-flop and bounce. Although the Batwing is now out of control, Batman manages to prise off the cockpit and this allows him to stagger out after the craft crashes into the Cathedral steps.

The Joker disappears into the Cathedral, with Vicki Vale as hostage, only to be followed by Batman. As The Joker skulks in the belfry and Batman speeds up the rotting stairs, only the bats overhead bear witness to the final confrontation...

HEARTS OF GOLD

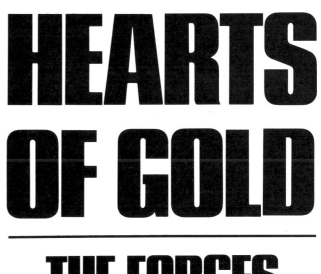

THE FORCES FOR GOOD

At times, the forces for good in this film seem as if they will be rubbed out forever by the crime and malevolence which sweep the city and hold it fast. Carl Grissom, Jack Napier and later, The Joker, can sneer from their high-rise luxury at the mortals below, secure in the knowledge that they have bought off the police and created a law for themselves. If Jack Napier causes Policeman Eckhardt's pockets to bulge with cash, or if he wants to murder an opponent, then who will stop him?

Commissioner Gordon, District Attorney Harvey Dent, and Mayor Borg, well intentioned to a man, seem capable of nothing more than empty speeches and are thrown into sharp relief by the gutsy will-power of Knox, the reporter, and Vicki Vale, the photo-journalist. Yet none can measure up to Batman himself who will dance in and out of the shadows, and so steer a beleaguered Gotham City back onto the course of true justice...

A tense moment unites the fearless twosome. In an attempt to escape the clutches of the Goons, Batman fires a grappling hook with spring action reel attachment from his speargun which he hopes will zip both Vicki and himself to the top of a high building.

37

MICHAEL KEATON'S

Unlike the square-jawed Batmans of the past, the normal-size Keaton reminds us that Batman is the only comic-book hero who is not a super-being. With an equal capacity for both comedy and drama, the star of **Beetlejuice** *is reunited with director Tim Burton.*

The clean-cut square-jaw of the television series was most certainly at odds with Tim Burton's vision of how Batman ought to look. Despite having given Michael Keaton the star role in *Beetlejuice*, it was, admits Tim, producers Jon Peters and Peter Guber who first suggested the actor.

Burton explains: 'There aren't many performers that when you look into their eyes you see a lot going on. And he is one of the few comedic actors who can bridge the gap to drama.' This may account for the appeal of what co-producer Chris Kenny calls his 'strangeness'.

Keaton's ability to blend comedy with drama at one and the same time clearly makes him an ideal choice as Batman who, Burton reminds us: 'is the one comic book hero who is not a superhero but a human being. Since Michael is hardly a big he-man, but looks just like a regular guy off the street, he was perfect for the role. Once he knew that my Batman wasn't going to be a great hulking brute, he liked the idea.'

Warner's themselves next realized that a musclebound powerhouse was not the requirement. Kim Bassinger actively approves the casting of Keaton; she asserts that she has not 'worked with anyone as wonderful as Michael. Along with Jack and Tim we were like "our gang", four children in the same playpen.'

Creating a non-bulky batman was clearly a challenge, yet Keaton has never shied away from risk. Of both *Beetlejuice* and *Clean and Sober* he said the following: 'These last two movies were choices that were real risky and absolutely right at a time when I should have been playing it as safe as I possibly could.'

Burton immediately creates the prevalent tone for the whole movie by introducing Batman from the start as a sinister vigilante. Cut off from the street world several hundred feet below, punks Eddie and Nick are squatting atop a tenement block after committing another thuggish crime. In the midst of a nervous conversation about 'the Bat', they hear a metallic clang and the sound of boots crunching on gravel.

BATMAN

Having selflessly sped Vicki to safety with the help of his spring action reel, Batman is now left alone in a dark alley to confront four Goons. As one of their number advances fearlessly with a sharp knife, another knocks Batman to the ground with a lead pipe. As the Goons gather round to prod and examine Batman, certain that they have dealt with the enemy, they are unprepared for the justice which he is about to mete out. Their unconscious bodies soon litter the alleyway.

Above: *Flanked by his limousine, dwarfed by his country home Wayne Manor, and dressed in smart clothes, Bruce Wayne suggests both his millionaire status and his easy authority.*

Right: *With their relationship now established, Bruce Wayne and Vicki Vale share a quiet moment within the safety of his luxury mansion.*

Frozen in their tracks, the muggers witness the approach of a threatening black figure, who flaps his great, shadowy wings in the wind. On his chest can be seen the emblem of a bat which is set against a yellow that glows in the dark. Referring to Nick in true vigilante style as 'Ratbreath', he metes out on-the-spot justice, before disappearing off into the night with alarming speed. As a result of this encounter, Eddie is left 'catatonic', and Nick 'brain-fried'.

Unlike any gangster, including Carl Grissom himself, Batman has the ability to frighten Jack Napier. In the Axis Chemical shoot-out, Napier successfully out-runs Commissioner Gordon and the entire police force by dint of his own fearlessness and a few handy vats of toxic waste. Spotting an escape route which will lead him to the East River and freedom, he dodges police gunfire but is clamped in a tight wrestling hold by Batman who has slipped out from the shadows. Napier is genuinely freaked out when he realizes who it is.

Batman is able to be both fearless and chivalrous at one and the same time. When he discovers that Vicki Vale is in the clutches of the Joker at the Flugelheim Museum, he thinks nothing of smashing through the skylight and, by means of a steel gauntlet, whisking her to freedom in great style. He also zips Vicki skywards on a wire, and disregards his own safety when he then has to dispense justice to The Joker's Goons.

BRUCE WAYNE

Batman's alter ego, Bruce Wayne, also has plenty of pluck. This is less easy to discern because of his busy brain which gives the impression of scattiness: he forgets the names of two of his party guests, as well as

Above left: *Decked out in smart coat, shirt and tie, Bruce Wayne looks suitably different from his alter ego Batman. Unlike Batman who hardly stands still for a second, Bruce has the relaxed and easy manner of the contented rich. His open face speaks of kindness, while his specs suggest the thoughtfulness that is a key character trait.*

Above: *With a poise that comes naturally to her, Vicki Vale can swtich from bomber jackets to tailored coat, while remaining equally elegant in either. Capable of both exuberance and introspection, she here ponders over the significance of the roses which Bruce has placed carefully in an alley.*

the society he's meant to be addressing.

Yet this handsome, 35-year-old millionaire fearlessly follows The Joker, after the latter has speared a fellow gang leader with a poisoned quill. He is also quick to indulge in some tough-talking with The Joker in Vicki's apartment, where he gives a sign of Batman's resourcefulness by fending off a bullet with a silver tray.

Adding to his complexity is that he can't find his socks without Alfred, while his kindly nature is evidenced by his generous gifts to humanitarian causes and by his impromptu grant to Knox the journalist.

Unlike all previous Batman adventures, where girlfriends, though they existed, never came too close, this picture embroils Bruce and Vicki Vale in a full sexual fling.

That he has been traumatized as a child by the murder of his parents is reason enough for him to lay down two long-stemmed roses in a deserted alleyway. It is an event which also explains Bruce's search, with the aid of his alter ego, for both himself and for universal justice. The greatest opponent in his search is The Joker. It was Jack Napier who, taking part himself in that distant childhood drama, gave Bruce Wayne a focus and an identity and so unwittingly created Batman; years later, it was Batman who returned the favour with interest when Jack Napier became The Joker.

As Batman tells The Joker at the end: 'I made you. And you made me.' One could not exist without the other, and their strange interdependence is a key to the movie.

BATMAN GETS HIS GIRL

Kim Basinger, whether the adventurous Eighties girl of *9½ Weeks* (1986) or the gutsy cowgirl of *Nadine* (1987), has never suggested even the slightest eccentricity. Yet Kim feels that her off-centre views and sympathy for the strange helped her work with Tim Burton, of whom she says, 'he's another freak – we both fly in the same way.' Their partnership, which relied on the shorthand language of close friends, helped her enormously in the role of Vicki Vale, which Kim 'was offered on a Friday and had to be there on the Monday.'

She had to instantly replace Sean Young, the original Vicki Vale, who fell off a horse and fractured a shoulder while rehearsing for the picture. Though she had no time whatsoever to think through the role, it was, she believes, 'the best thing that could have happened. The slate was wiped clean and it was up to me to interpret the character.'

Director Tim Burton bounces with enthusiasm as he delivers a eulogy on Basinger, who also gained admirers in *No Mercy* (1986) and *Blind Date* (1987). 'I've got to hand it to Kim. It can't have been easy to join a movie which we'd already started shooting. Kim has added a lot to it. She has a positive, "let's get going" attitude which is also very much part of the Vicki Vale character. In short, she has been great for the movie.'

Mark Canton, President of Worldwide Motion Picture Production for Warner Bros., is equally complimentary about Kim. 'Kim is funny, sexy, a real pro. She is also a generous cheerleader who gives a lot to the rest of the cast. I now can't imagine anyone else as Vicki Vale'.

VICKI VALE

Far from being just a means of occupying Bruce Wayne during his spare time ('he has a girlfriend so he does have his off hours!'), Vicki Vale is truly independent and proves herself, according to Kim, to be 'gutsy, enterprising, modern and adventurous. She also possesses a lot of truth and honesty and stands up for what she believes in.'

She has certainly spared no effort in capturing brutally honest photographs of the grimmest war-zones. During her first appearance in the picture, in the offices of the Gotham Globe, a reporter colleague called Knox admires her combat portfolio as well as her striking legs. Only a girl with the confidence to dress as a fashionable

Above: *Much can be gleaned about Vicki's character from her appearance which varies throughout the film. Here, dressed for a party at Bruce Wayne's mansion, she is the picture of grace, femininity and self-control.*

Right: *By contrast, Vicki proves her pluck when out on the road with Batman. Although dishevelled, perspiring and exhausted, she never loses her alertness.*

individual would have the nerve to film exploding jeeps, burning huts and piles of bodies. From the start, she is seen as an easy match for the cocky Knox, and their relationship is cemented as much by free-wheeling banter as by mutual trust and admiration. Their joint wit is evidence of their quick intelligence and up-front confidence.

Certainly Vicki is well up to tackling Bruce Wayne, who, as a charming millionaire, might well intimidate anyone who meets him for the first time. Aside from joking with him about his exotic sword collection, she also suggests cheekily that he might be as idle as he is rich – he has yet to reveal himself as Batman.

The two soon experience a close encounter of the first kind, which highlights just how much Bruce Wayne has changed. Although conceived by Bob Kane as a ladies' man, he had never been less than chivalrous towards

any of his girlfriends. Now, through Vicki, he is propelled into the Eighties, and is filmed lying next to her on the pillow. Bruce Wayne in bed with a woman! Their relationship is also a handy means of developing the more human side of Batman, which is used to balance his role as a sinister avenger.

But Vicki's hard-nosed curiosity leads her to discover Bruce Wayne's deepest secret and the reason for his disguise as Batman. Her fearlessness finally allows her to be as unafraid of falling in love with Bruce as it does to pick her way through a panic-stricken crowd in the final sequence. Here she proves her pluck by jumping into the driving seat of Knox's car, so as to save Knox himself from near certain death. Vicki Vale's pluck is nearly her undoing when she is captured by The Joker in the final sequence. He takes her into the bell tower as bait for Batman but she is safe in the knowledge that Batman will make very effort to save her.

Above: *Just like Batman himself, Vicki Vale is often in the thick of danger. Seen here in the evil grip of a Goon, she is prevented from speaking and can only cry out for help with her eyes.*

Left: *With the physical and mental agility needed for her job as a photo-journalist, Vicki seldom wastes a second in her search for the perfect shot.*

HEARTS OF GOLD

THE GENTLEMEN'S GENTLEMAN

The one individual who represents an oasis of calm in amongst the action, anxiety and high-jinks, is Alfred, professional Englishman and butler to Bruce Wayne. Like Knox, a means of allowing levity and wit as much room in the film as intensity and disaster, he is the means by which Bruce Wayne's day-to-day life is beautifully ordered.

Fleshed out wonderfully by English actor, Michael Gough, he is mannered without being stiff, and humorous without being frivolous. He also succeeds in exuding warmth while keeping his proper distance. Gough speaks affectionately of his role as Alfred the butler: 'I feel I'm the nanny. I don't have to change his diaper, but I do have to do pretty much everything else. Alfred doesn't have to act like a butler. He *is* the butler, one of nature's gentlemen.'

With his 'dry sense of humour', he is able to joke with Bruce's party guests but without ever patronizing them. With his polished manners, Alfred contrasts well with the bluff Knox, who turns up to the party and says to him: 'You know, if you cut your bathroom in half, you'd have my whole apartment.'

Right from the outset, Alfred's discretion is revealed. Clearly indicating that he is conversant with Bruce's double life, he guides him from the party to the Batcave with a wink and a nudge. He has, in fact, been a surrogate father to Bruce since the latter was a mere child. He instinctively understands what makes his charge tick and is always around to help at just the right moment.

He not only tiptoes gently into the Batcave when Bruce is asleep, in order to fold his Bat-cape, but is also capable of giving Bruce some fatherly advice about Vicki Vale: 'If I may say so, she is really quite special. Perhaps you could try telling her the truth.'

Below left: *As the only man who knows of Bruce Wayne's double identity, Alfred the butler is always at hand to help the fight against crime. Here Alfred is deep inside the Batcave selecting a cape from his master's wardrobe.*

Below: *A surrogate father to Batman since the latter was a boy, Alfred is always ready to meet every demand and satisfy every whim, but is unafraid to offer pointed advice as well. He is the perfect blend of sympathy and strength.*

OPPORTUNITY KNOX

Knox is played by Robert Wuhl, actor, comedian, writer and director, who is best known as the disc jockey who played opposite Robin Williams in *Good Morning Vietnam* (1988). Wuhl projects not only the right air of moon-faced innocence and obsessive single-mindedness, but also the kind of infectious schoolboy enthusiasm which sweeps Vicki along too.

Attributing his appearance in the film to 'Tim Burton's momentary loss of senses', Wuhl confirms that 'Knox knows it's a big story, knows he's right, and doesn't care if no-one believes him.' Wuhl believes that 'journalists the world over will love Knox. No editors believe him. He's up against a rich guy and he gets to romance Kim Basinger'.

Above and left: *Knox is the cavalier journalist who truly believes in the existence of Batman but has to put up with office mockery as a result. With regulation raincoat and newspaper jammed in his pocket, he is the epitome of the hard-nosed reporter who will defy both authority and colleagues in his quest for truth.*

Very much the stylized maverick which Hollywood created as its preferred kind of reporter, Knox lives up to the tradition as, in Wuhl's words, 'a wise-cracking smart-ass'.

A fan of DC comics but not of the TV series, which he finds 'too campy', Wuhl prepared for the movie role studying the day-to-day workings of reporters on the New York *Daily News*.

In the film, Knox positively froths with enthusiasm when he discovers that Vicki too has faith in the existence of Batman. It is the closeness of Knox and Vicki which permits the lightweight banter and punchy wit that act as a foil to the darker aspects of the story. Even when Knox finds himself jealous of Bruce because of Vicki's interest in him, he never allows it to dent his confidence so that he loses sight of his goal. Instead, he kills off jealousy by letting fly some fun jokes and witty one-liners. Yet, his determination is suitably solemn when on his mission to find Batman and he is even prepared to risk his life in the quest. During the mayhem towards the end of the movie when the Joker is about to puncture his poison balloons, Knox finds himself clinging for his life to the front of a speeding car driven by Vicki Vale.

THE FORCES OF LAW AND ORDER

Knox certainly has more know-how and courage than Commissioner Gordon (Pat Hingle), District Attorney Harvey Dent (Billy Dee Williams) and Mayor Borg (Lee Wallis), who are portrayed as well-meaning bureaucrats. The worn-out speeches of this righteous threesome points to their ineffectual efforts to clean up the town.

Like a true politico, Mayor Borg loves to speechify: 'Across the nation, the name Gotham City is synonymous with crime. Our streets are over-run, and our police officials have been helpless. As Mayor, I promised you that I would root out the source of corruption – Boss Karl Grissom! Our new District Attorney, Harvey Dent, will carry out that promise. I promise.'

Dent is no better, and while insisting that 'although a man of few words, these words will count', declares his intention 'to shed the light of the law on that nest of vipers.'

That Bruce Wayne is the only one absent from this meeting at the Gotham City Democrats Club is a means of highlighting the empty noise of officialdom, while suggesting that Wayne, as his alter-ego Batman, is probably sliding through the night as a one-man avenger to actually solve Gotham's endemic crime.

Knox amusingly points out the stupidity of the officials by irritating them with talk of Batman at Bruce Wayne's party. Gordon's authority is also seen to be crumbling, because of the antics of one of his subordinates, Eckhardt, who is not only tucked safely in Napier's pocket, but is also leading a full-scale operation against the gang without referring upwards to the Commissioner. The Dent-Gordon solution is to cling to their misguided plan for a 200th Anniversary party for Gotham City whose PR gloss, they hope, will rid the citizens of their fears about their town and its hoodlums.

COMMISSIONER GORDON

Gotham City has become a plaything in the hands of Carl Grissom and Jack Napier. Its citizens are mere puppets who exist to serve the criminal whims of the two gangsters. Yet it is The Joker who will particularly try the patience of Commissioner Gordon who is here asserting himself fully in his war against crime. Although depicted as a burly figure of authority, he will later learn that only Batman can truly squash lawbreakers underfoot.

DISTRICT ATTORNEY HARVEY DENT

A sharp-suited attorney who is as well attired as Jack Napier, Harvey Dent has the same righteous aims as Gordon, but is overwhelmed by the trickery of Grissom's gang.

MAYOR BORG

Here depicted as a thoughtful man, the beleaguered Mayor Borg has plenty to consider as he plans ways of sweeping gangsters off the streets for good. On the same side as Dent and Gordon, Borg will soon reap the benefit of the Caped Crusader.

SOULS OF BLACK

THE FORCES OF EVIL

Bob Kane always made sure that Batman's physical strength and quickness of mind were put to the test by a battery of villains. The Penguin, Catwoman, Punch and Judy and Two-Face all contributed to the threatening tone of the early comics. The television series, however, turned criminals into clowns who caused laughter rather than fear.

In both comics and television The Joker was the enemy par excellence. With his violent green hair, ghoulish make-up and freaky grin, he gave off the compulsive combination of both evil and fun.

Left: *Even with his handy flesh-tone make-up, The Joker cannot disguise his manic laugh and malicious intent.*

Above: *Whether dominating gangland or simply playing cards, Jack Napier's vanity requires him to be the best-dressed thug around.*

Right: *Jack Nicholson, his Joker make-up in disarray, with producer Jon Peters. Peters was instrumental in casting Nicholson as The Joker.*

NICHOLSON'S JOKER

*Green hair • White face • Blood red lips • Two hours to apply make-up, one hour to
remove it • Flesh-tone make-up enables The Joker to look semi-normal, but with manic
grin still intact • Screaming outfits • Broad brimmed fedora • Several screws loose*

Tim Burton has pitted The Joker against Batman in the new movie and chosen well in Jack Nicholson. Producer Jon Peters, who knew Jack from *The Witches of Eastwick* (1987), talked long and hard to Nicholson in order to convince him to accept the role.

Right from the off, all concerned with the movie believed that Jack had to be The Joker. Kim Basinger herself admits that 'Jack has a lot of The Joker in him', while Mark Canton concurs that 'Jack related to Tim's vision of the picture.' Burton himself agrees that 'Jack Nicholson is that character, no question about it. He is so right and was constantly thought of at the planning stage.'

Co-producer Chris Kenny says that the start of shooting was put back to accommodate Jack, but knows that it was worthwhile: 'The minute he comes on, the set lights up.' Despite the grind of a tough schedule, Nicholson had, according to Mark Canton, President of Worldwide Production, 'a ball on the movie. He very much took the lead and constantly helped the others.'

Brian Hammond was one of the extras on the film. One of the last mavericks in London's Soho, he runs Gerry's drinking club with the help of his wife Dee and a large beard. Gerry's is a favourite haunt of many actors, and Brian has met quite a few in his time behind the bar. He has nothing but praise for Nicholson on set, and refers to him as 'good-natured, supportive and terribly professional. He was very good to us extras and would always crack a joke when he made a mistake.'

Kim Basinger refers to Batman, The Joker and Vicki Vale as three kindred spirits or, as she more colourfully puts it, 'three strange entities looking for some place to land'.

Certainly The Joker scores top marks for strangeness. As Jack Napier (his identity before the grisly transformation), he is introduced as arrogant, malevolent and extremely vain. Our first sight of him is via a close-up of his hand which is long, thin and manicured; this adds an interesting twist to our perceived image of a murdering thug.

Far left: *Shaking hands with The Joker is rarely a sign of friendship. Here, gangster Rotelli, who has dared voice an opinion, is fried to a crisp at a mob meeting.*

Centre: *The Joker smiles salaciously over a picture of Vicki Vale whom he sees here for the first time.*

Left: *In the midst of mayhem at Gotham City's 200th anniversary parade, only The Joker gloats over proceedings with customary arrogance.*

His obsessive vanity and acute dress-sense are all part of his crude attempt to forget that he is no longer a fancy-free teenager.

Lounging in the apartment of Grissom's girlfriend, Alicia (with whom he is having an affair), he arrogantly rests his feet on a picture of his lover which is gracing the cover of *Vogue*. Seemingly regarding her only as a plaything, and certainly ignoring everything she says, his eyes dart constantly from a TV screen to a nearby mirror in which he can't stop admiring himself. Before he leaves the apartment, he runs a hand through his well-groomed hair and checks his tailored suit. With Napier, arrogance and insecurity go hand-in-hand.

During an alley-way altercation with Eckhardt, it is the policeman who points to the more sinister aspects of Napier's make-up. After asserting that he answers to Grissom 'not to psychos', Eckhardt further makes his point, as follows: 'You got no future Jack. You're an A-1 nut, boy, and Grissom know it.'

Instinctively cruel to boot, Napier clamps his hand on the back of Eckhardt's head and shoves him into a wall. After Napier's accident gives him a new face and so turns him into The Joker, his lust for power is as strong as ever, and, by shooting Grissom dead, he is able to give it full vent. The one objector in Grissom's mob literally disappears in smoke while The Joker's Goons have their uniforms restyled by their new leader. If clothes maketh the man, then goodness knows what the Goons are wearing. Still, a dash of green here and a touch of purple there seem as important to The Joker as money and power.

Though he can hide his intentions under a perfectly fitting zoot-suit, The Joker can't

always conceal his new bleached-out face under his flesh-tone make-up. While laying down the law to his fellow gang leaders, he begins to sweat, the flesh-tone flows and the alarming graveyard pallor is on view for everyone to see.

Even when alone, The Joker likes to indulge his love of cruelty. His lair in the bowels of Axis Chemicals is decorated with photographs of dead soldiers, whose crazy grins are the result of experimental nerve gas.

Bruce's official file on The Joker reveals that when only 15 years old, he committed assault with a deadly weapon. Psychological tests revealed a high IQ, but an unstable temperament, as well as a keen interest in art.

Confronting Vicki in the Flugelheim Museum, he casts his eyes over her photos (he only likes the war-zone horror-shots), before calling on his twisted charm to try and convince her that crime itself is an art form.

The Joker's instability and malice propel his sense of fun. He is never more amused than when life is in danger, particularly from himself. Dizzy with the opportunity which the Gotham City 200th anniversary parade will give him, he plans to celebrate by gassing the population of Gotham City. He shrieks to Batman with great pleasure: 'I'm going to the festival. You really ought to show up. I'm

gonna to kill a thousand people an hour until you do.'

At the parade, the disco blast from The Joker's giant speakers feeds his frenzy, while he simultaneously reveals the hypocrisy of the townspeople. Those who complain about his bully-boy tactics now display the same baseness as The Joker himself, by scrambling around for money which the villain is dispensing with the help of his Goons.

The only real hint that The Joker's crazed laughter may just be a veil concealing a life of pain comes during an earlier encounter with Bruce and Vicki: 'I'm only laughing on the outside', he says. 'My smile is just skin-deep. If you could see that inside I'm really crying, you might join me for a weep.'

Above: *With gleeful malice, The Joker is happy to front one of his own television commercials which show the wide range of poisoned products now on offer.*

Right: *The graveyard pallor, which resulted from The Joker's accident at Axis Chemical can do nothing to conceal his ever-active mind which is already planning his next nasty move.*

GRUESOME GRISSOM

Until his emergence as The Joker puts him on the throne, Jack Napier is ruled over by Carl Grissom, a lantern-jawed charmer who dwarfs all around him. It is Jack Palance who turns in a marvellous performance as the gangland brute. Tim Burton comments on the problem of casting Grissom:

'Because Jack Nicholson is such a strong, cinematic figure, there aren't many you can imagine as his boss, but Jack Palance fills out the role perfectly, and is, in fact, able to make Nicholson look like a kid at times'.

Dominating his penthouse apartment with, naturally, the best view of Gotham City, Grissom is fawned over not only by square-headed goons, but also by spineless toadies who cater to his every malicious whim. He rarely needs to leave the safety of his apartment, since he relies on others to carry out his robberies and killings for him.

Left: *With a natural air of authority, and a physical bulk to match, gang boss Carl Grissom rules Gotham City – for the moment.*

Top: *Without the least idea that his mainman Jack Napier smells a set up and will soon fill his shoes, Grissom convinces him that he ought to personally take charge of the Axis Chemical operation.*

Above: *Tim Burton has mentioned the difficulty of casting an actor who would look convincing on screen as Jack Nicholson's boss. Here, actor Jack Palance is able to make Carl Grissom dwarf everything in his apartment.*

Because he suspects Napier of double-dealing, Grissom insists that his chief side-kick personally mounts the dangerous Axis Chemical Factory operation and so tries to set him up to be caught by the cops.

Yet even Grissom can panic. On his return from the Axis mission, Napier (now The Joker) barges into his boss's apartment, frightens him with his new face, and gives him the benefit of a loaded gun. As The Joker exclaims much later in the film: 'I'm prepared to rule the world!!'

ALICIA THE GANGSTER'S MOLL

The one individual who both unites – and eventually divides – the two thugs is Alicia Hunt (Jerry Hall). Depicted as a traditional gangster's moll, both feisty and passive, she is supposedly loyal to Carl Grissom, but thinks nothing of spending time with Jack Napier.

She is also a young, beautiful model. Her apartment is spattered with photographs of herself which indicate a narcissism that is an even match for Jack's. Her many shopping bags effectively bolster the image.

Jerry Hall took to the part because, as she says, 'Alicia is on the bad side – she is in with some really bad guys. Although primarily naughty, she also has a certain innocence.' A fan of the Batman TV series as a youngster, Jerry was delighted to be offered the role which came her way in chance circumstances. At Pinewood to shoot a commercial, she met Peter Young, the set decorator.

'I was on a 15-minute break, and saw the sun filtering through a window in a corridor. I went to take a look. Peter ran into me and that's how I got the part'. Tim Burton himself speaks approvingly: 'If Jerry were to play just a model, it would be a simple cameo but I wanted to give her an interesting part.'

Top and above: *Grissom's girlfriend Alicia, a top Gotham City model, finds no difficulty in sharing her favours with Jack Napier. Dressed as expensively as Jack, she is possessed of a vanity which is an equal match for her lovers and allows her to go on constant shopping sprees.*

Above: *The perfect pairing of two outsize egos. Here The Joker sits smugly in Alicia's apartment, which is modestly decked out with photographs of herself.*

Right: *Her good looks will, however, soon be blotted out by a nasty acid accident.*

In the film, Alicia is treated appallingly by Jack Napier. Not content with frightening her silly with his new look, he flings acid in her face so that she acquires one too. She now has to wear a porcelain doll's mask to hide the disfigurement, and take pills to ease the pain. Her transformation is revealed to Vicki Vale at the Flugelheim and the normally level-headed photo-journalist goes into deep shock.

Her disfigurment plays with our received notion of the model as unblemished. Burton is quick to agree: 'Sure, a recognisable figure like Jerry Hall with a scar is interesting.'

Jerry says she herself was 'a little disturbed when it came to make-up. I had scars over and under my eyes, as well as on my neck and mouth. There were bumps everywhere, and skin was left hanging from my jaw.'

She describes Alicia's relationship to Napier as so warped that 'she persists in staying with him, even though he has disfigured her. She follows him like a dog. In keeping with the relationship, he calls himself "Daddy".' Jerry sees Alicia and Napier as having 'one of the all-time sick relationships. I used to say to Jack on set, "It's a sick relationship, but it works!"' It is refreshing to learn that the relationship between Hall and Nicholson is extremely healthy. Aside from giving Jerry 'many wonderful acting tips', Jack is also her son's godfather and his partner, Angelica Huston, the godmother.

FROM HOODS TO ...

Left: *The Goons's cartoon-style outfits never obscure the fact that they provide a vicious back-up to The Joker. Here they dominate a scene of mayhem on the Cathedral steps of Gotham City.*

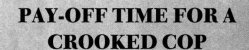

*The mean, fat face of Eckhardt is fitting for
a corrupt cop who takes easy money from
Jack Napier.*

Eckhardt (William Hootkins) is the only link
between right and wrong. Nominally an
integral member of Commissioner Gordon's
crime-fighters, he has long since been
bought off by Grissom for a fat fee. With no
conscience whatsoever, he flits in and out of
both worlds depending on his current needs.
He is the ultimate cynic and complete
pragmatist.

Introduced early in the action, he reveals
himself as an unfeeling hard-nut. As punks
Eddie and Nick, who have been scared
witless by Batman, pass by on stretchers on
their way to a waiting ambulance, Eckhardt
remarks: 'They're all drinkin' Drano', before
amusing himself with the quip: 'Sorry, Knox.
These two slipped on a banana peel.'

However, the man who thinks nothing of
usurping the authority of Commissioner
Gordon can still be petrified by Napier.
During their alleyway encounter, when
Napier passes the corrupt cop a paper bag
crammed with cash, Eckhardt receives a
severe pounding and so leaves the scene
driven by terror. He has just cause for this
since it is Napier who finally puts Eckhardt to
death during the Axis shoot-out.

..... GOONS

Above: *With his outsize vanity, The Joker has
developed as keen an interest in natty clothes as he
has in killer crimes. His new role as gang leader
has allowed him to restyle the Goons who here
resemble a group of loopy Frenchmen.*

61

MODEL ACTION

VISUAL EFFECTS

Derek Meddings is the last person to worry if he is ignored. As, visual effects supervisor on Batman, he takes it as a compliment if audiences take the intricacies of his art for granted.

Meddings is a veteran of five Bond films, as well as the *Superman* series. He was, in fact, awarded a special effects Oscar for his work on the first *Superman* film. More pertinently, with regard to Batman, he designed a strange assortment of craft for the ground−breaking 'Thunderbirds' TV series and is still regularly invited to attend cult seminars the world over.

DEREK MEDDINGS

A veteran of five Bond films, Derek Meddings also won an Oscar for his work on the first Superman film. He also designed the model craft for 'Thunderbirds'.

His early days working with Gerry and Sylvia Anderson, Derek feels, taught him a lot: 'It helped a great deal. We crashed cars and planes and undertook complex street scenes. In fact, I tried most of what you see in *Batman* during my time with 'Thunderbirds'. During this time I developed a particular feeling for aircraft.'

ON A BATWING AND A PRAYER

This has proved particularly useful in relation to the tricky Batwing sequences, one of which sees the craft crash onto Broad Avenue, skid and bump along the street, and end up on the Cathedral steps. The Batwing, disappeared in a ball of flame.

In this sequence, the problem was two-fold. Given that, according to Meddings, staging an aircraft crash is always complicated, 'it becomes harder when the plane is completely fictional. You have to try even more to make the action look convincing.' Secondly, this particular scene (which was shot on a one-twelfth scale miniature set) had to blend seamlessly with a live-action version of the same event.

'They had positioned a large section of the wrecked Batwing on the Cathedral steps. We had to place our model in *precisely* the same position. To ensure it broke up, we made it out of pewter which is a nice, soft metal.' Because of the shooting speed (very quick, at 120 frames per second), it is, says Derek, very tough to take in every detail of the action on the monitors. 'You only really know what you've got when you see the rushes the following day. A mixture of clever cutting and spot-on camera angles means that you really can't see the joins.'

Left: *Derek has very successfully created in miniature the brutal hostility of Gotham City's main street which is a playground for gangsters.*

Above: *The Batwing, designed by Anton Furst, was constructed as a model by Derek and his team. Only one section of the craft, seen here burning on the Cathedral steps, was completed in full-scale.*

Above: *Aside from The Batmobile, Batman's only other vehicle of attack is The Batwing. Deliberately designed after the sickle-shape of the Bat-symbol, it slices through the air at great speed.*

THE

Main Picture: *Veering quickly, yet carefully, over the main street, Batman prepares to use his high-tech weaponry to wipe out The Joker.*

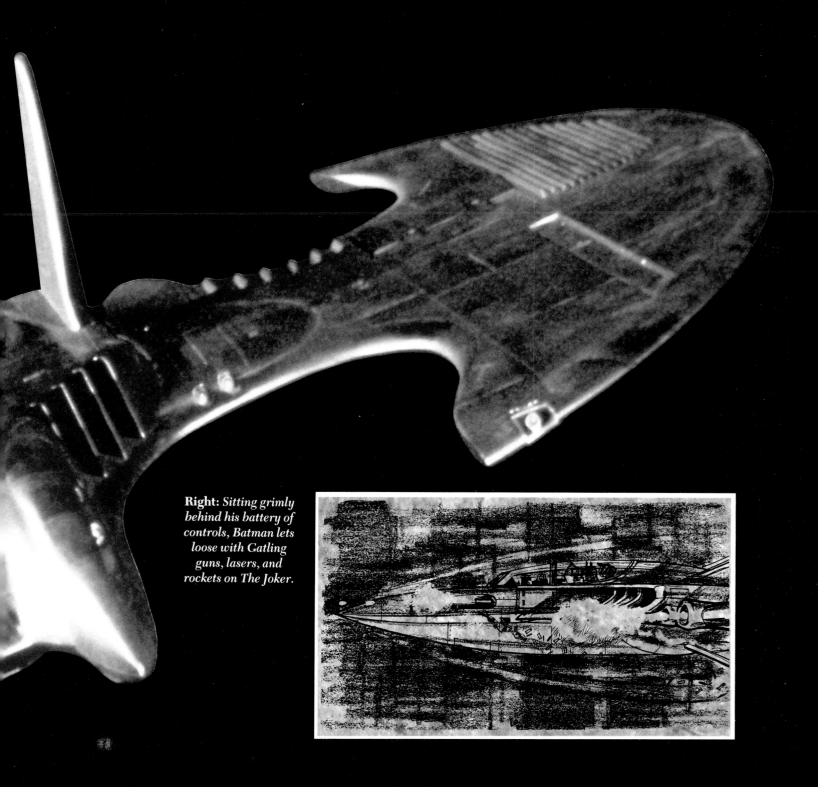

Right: *Sitting grimly behind his battery of controls, Batman lets loose with Gatling guns, lasers, and rockets on The Joker.*

BATWING TAKES OFF

Designed by Anton Furst after the sickle-shaped Bat-symbol • Armaments – rockets, gatling guns (two), lasers • Performance details unknown • Never been seen at ground level

BATMAN CRANES HIS
HEAD FORWARD & LOOKS
DOWN & FRONT
(FULL ART STREET PLATE)

1

Hunched for action
in the cockpit of the
Batwing, Batman
homes in on The Joker.

THE NOSE LIFTS WITH
NOTHING - TO - SPARE.

2

Batman has to fly the
Batwing on the limit in
order to avoid a head-
on smash with Gotham
City's 1,000 foot-high
Cathedral.

3

With finger on the
trigger, Batman
prepares to unleash his
up-to-date arsenal on
The Joker.

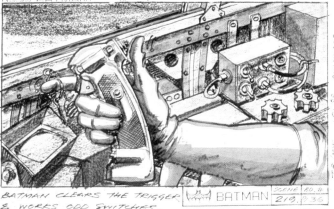

BATMAN CLEARS THE TRIGGER
& WORKS ODD SWITCHES,
ETC.

THE JOKER UNDER ATTACK

It was equally difficult to film another scene involving the Batwing. To capture the craft swooping towards the city centre as Batman mounts an attack on The Joker, it was necessary to build a special motion-control camera for the scale set. The camera had to duck and dive around an 18-foot (5.5m) set, which was cluttered with oddly angled buildings, themselves grouped closely around a street that was only 10 inches (25cm) wide. Thus, an overhead camera which could move right in on the action was an essential item.

Reminding us that his unit not only creates the effects but also films them, and despite the assistance of four camermen, Derek still speaks nervously of tough camera angles in this sequence. Making their way through The Joker's floats, searchlight lorries and a maze of traffic, the cameras had to shoot exactly what Batman sees from the craft. It was particularly difficult to film the Batwing as it banked up behind the cathedral before the final assault on The Joker.

MICHAEL WHITE

Unlike most production designers, whose drawings are often more like rough sketches, Anton Furst insists on fully detailed pencil drawings of all his designs. They are, in fact, works of art which would not be out of place in an art gallery. Veteran storyboard artist Michael White (right) is drawing a wonderfully detailed cityscape in which the intense clutter of buildings creates the correct sense of claustrophobia and oppression. Michael has brought to these drawings a track record of substance which includes *A Bridge Too Far* (1977), *Gandhi* (1982), *Superman IV* (1987), and *Who Framed Roger Rabbit* (1988).

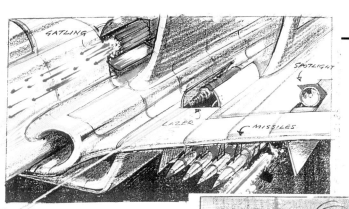

THE BATWING OPENS-UP WITH EVERYTHING.

4

Assisted by a spotlight to pick out his target, Batman lets fly with laser and Gatling guns, as well as a volley of missiles.

JOKER AVOIDS A MISSILE AND EVERYTHING ELSE!

5

Leaping in the manic style which comes naturally to him, The Joker dodges each projectile and so lives on to mock his assailant.

THE BATWING BELLY-FLOPS ONTO THE STREET &, BOUNCES OUT OF FRAME IT TRAILS BLACK SMOKE, ETC.

6

Knocked off course by a bullet from The Joker, the Batwing belly-flops onto Broad Avenue and bounces towards the Cathedral.

BLOW-UP MODELS

Derek's son Mark was largely responsible for the model buildings. Based strongly on the surreal designs of Anton Furst, the movie's production designer, they punch out an

Above: *To convincingly film the many sharp and awkward corners of Gotham City, Derek Meddings found it necessary to build a special motion control camera rig.*

eclectic mixture of styles which range from Gothic to Art Deco, high-tech industrial to Brutalism. Constructed in wood, perspex and fibre-glass, they were built in the tiniest detail in only a matter of months. They are reductions of buildings which, on the screen, are more than 800 ft (244m) high, while the Cathedral itself is over 1,000 ft (305m).

Derek here explains the problem of looking at the set through both the naked eye and the camera itself. 'When we first shot the city centre, it just didn't look right and I couldn't work out why. I soon realised that, even though they were varnished, the streets looked dull. The answer was to spray them with oil, which we also used to highlight sections of the vehicles.'

DESIGNED FOR DESTRUCTION

Providing an equal technical challenge was the scene centred on the destruction of the Axis Chemical Factory. This included a split picture in which the bottom half (live-action) depicts the Batmobile pulling out of the plant, while the top half (matching model) shows the factory exploding.

'We were again shooting at high speed, 120 frames per second. Because it is quite hard to make a building collapse in just the way you want, it was necessary to have breakaway plaster sections so that the right chunks of the building exploded. Because we had to let off a series of explosions very quickly, it made sense to use a striker-board which allows you that possibility. You also have to be careful that the interior of the building looks real, because you can, of course, see it after the explosion.'

The forbidding brutalism of the Axis Chemical Factory disappears for good in the midst of a splendid orange fireball. Carefully timed explosions were the result of imaginative preparation by the special and visual effects teams.

BIG BANGS AND BATGADGETS

SPECIAL EFFECTS

Another member of the crew who is equally concerned with creating an appearance of realism is special effects supervisor, John Evans. The man who contributed the dazzling effects for *Moonwalker* (1988), *Octopussy* (1983) and *Full Metal Jacket* (1987) is especially proud of the Batmobile whose presence in the workshop ensured that 'this was the only time I can remember my boys coming in early!'

A long-serving team of 12 all-round technicians (who can switch readily from detailed electronics to heavy welding) built the Batmobile in a mere 12 weeks. John and his team created a machine which captures the nightmare quality of Anton Furst's design. Almost 20ft long and 8ft wide (6m x 2.5m), its dramatically curved, black fibre-glass shell fits the gloomy tone of a film which returns Batman to his earliest role as an urban crime-fighter.

'I wanted the Batmobile to look timeless,' claims Anton Furst. 'I didn't want a futuristic vehicle on a pastiche 1950s car. I went for the most brutal expression of a car, an image which also suggests sex and violence.'

Almost a symbol for Tim Burton's intention to restore the threatening world of the earliest Batman, the Batmobile gives off a brooding air of purposeful malice and streaks through the streets like a killer bullet. It possesses the same sinister sleekness of Batman himself and contains within its black body an array of gadgets and weapons which Batman uses to clear a path for justice. The crew is seen here filming the explosion at Axis Chemical which the car has set off in order to cripple The Joker's operations.

Wheels – 24ins (60cm) radius.
Specially for drag-racing.
Imported from the USA.

THE BATMOBILE

Body and power unit – a heady mixture of a Blue Riband Utah Flats speed machine and Formula One Grand Prix racer combined with the staying power of a Centurion tank • Speed – 90 mph in 5 seconds • Fuel consumption – only for the mega-rich • Two Browning machine guns • A grappling hook, which will grab the nearest building, shoots out from right nearside the assist the Batmobile to take corners at speed • A 24-volt system, built into the car, powers all the gadgets

Burner – fuelled by gas and
paraffin mix.

Body – all fibreglass.
Length – 19ft 6ins (5.9m)
Width – 8ft (2.4m)

It is astonishing to realise that the high-tech sleekness of the new Batmobile came together so quickly. Based on a design by production designer Anton Furst, its dramatically curved fibreglass shell dropped perfectly at first attempt onto pre-stretched customised chassis components. From the first glance it took only 12 weeks to build.

With two Browning machine guns unexpectedly concealed beneath flaps in each wing, and with crab-like claw at the front for added danger, the Batmobile's aura of purposeful malice befits a film which has removed Batman himself from the comic books and returned him to his early role as an urban crime fighter.

ACTION AT AXIS CHEMICAL

John comes up with a catalogue of detail concerning the explosion of Axis Chemical, one of the key scenes involving the Batmobile. 'Tim Burton wanted to go for full-size, 100-feet flames. You couldn't get within 50 feet of them. We wired up thousands of sandbags, pumped gas through galvanised piping and safely set the explosives in steel cases. The trick was to drive the car through all this before it melted!'

While the Axis interior was shot at a run-down building in Acton, West London, the exploding exterior was filmed at a derelict power-station in the rural setting of Little Barford. At a cost of 3,000-4,000 per tanker, 45 tonnes of liquid gas were used, an amount which, according to Evans, 'would heat a 20-30 house village for a whole year!'

Right: *Causing both fear and amazement as it races through the city, the Batmobile is here hurtling towards the Batcave.*

Below: *Ignoring the Goons' bullets which have no hope of puncturing its full metal jacket, the Batmobile enters Axis Chemical in order to destroy it.*

John points to the two and a half weeks of imaginative preparation and hard work which are required to bring to life a mere half minute of screen time. He highlights his close-working relationship with Anton Furst: 'Engineering and design are very close. If a problem is related to engineering rather than design, Anton passes it over to me. If it's a design worry, I go to Anton.'

Like Derek Meddings, Evans makes the point that so much of his work remains unseen; the so-called gimbals which enable the Batwing to weave like a plane, or the tricks he invents to enable an otherwise immobile Bat-cape to flow with style. So many of these problems, invisible to an audience, require a great deal of lateral thought.

BATMAN VERSUS THE JOKER

BATMAN'S WEAPONS

Multi-purpose utility belt
Speargun
Steel gauntlet
Ninja wheels
Batarangs

The gadgets which enable Batman to fight for justice are all designed by John Evans and his team. Batman's utility belt houses an array of handy items which include Ninja wheels, Batarangs and a speargun. The Ninja wheels prove useful to stun an opponent, a Batarang helps whizz Vicki Vale to safety, while the multi-purpose speargun ensnares a Goon at Axis Chemical.

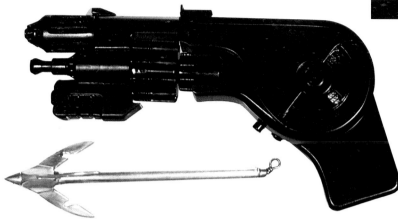

THE SPEARGUN

The speargun, which also fires grappling hooks, was, according to Evans, 'extremely complicated for us. Small, stream-lined gadgets are tough, especially when they have to be functional as well. In this case we had to accommodate two-inch motors in the gun.'

THE GAUNTLET

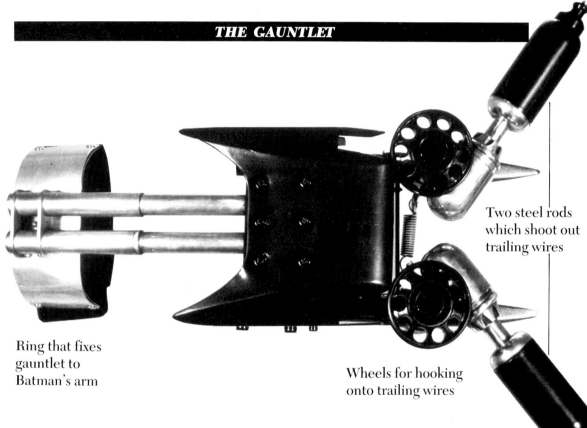

Ring that fixes gauntlet to Batman's arm

Two steel rods which shoot out trailing wires

Wheels for hooking onto trailing wires

JOHN EVANS

Much of John Evans' work remains invisible to an audience: like the Batwing or with the Batcloak. However, only too visible is John's spendid Batmobile, which he built with the aid of his twelve-man team, all of whom can switch at ease from detailed electronics to heavy welding. John himself contributed the knock-out special effects for *Moonraker* (1979), *Octopussy* (1983), *Raiders of the Lost Ark* (1981) and *Full Metal Jacket* (1987).

THE UTILITY BELT

The Ninja wheels (thrown to great effect by Batman) are made of aluminium when seen, and fibreglass when not. The wheels, part of Batman's state-of-the-art toolbox, fit neatly onto his utility belt, which Evans felt ought to move: 'Again, this was hard to achieve. By means of a motorized chain inside the belt, Batman is able to zip an item round from back to front. This adds to the drama, of course, but we also felt he would look like a Marine if all the gadgets were clamped to his front. Again, this is a case of ten days' detailed preparation making two seconds of screen time.'

One high-tech gadget, written in at the start is the steel gauntlet which Batman employs at the Flugelheim Museum to speed Vicki to safety. It has two guns which fire two steel rods which shoot out trailing wires. The gauntlet itself turns into a wheel which in turn hooks onto the trailing wires and helps Batman and Vicki escape from the clutches of The Joker.

John explains the design challenge here: 'The gauntlet really should have been 18-20 in [50cm] long in order to take the weight, but, to keep it in scale, and to enable it to fit Batman's belt, we had to reduce it to 9 in [25cm] and still make it safe'. Evans points out that part of his job is 'instilling confidence in actors when they're 50-60 ft [16cm] up on a wire'.

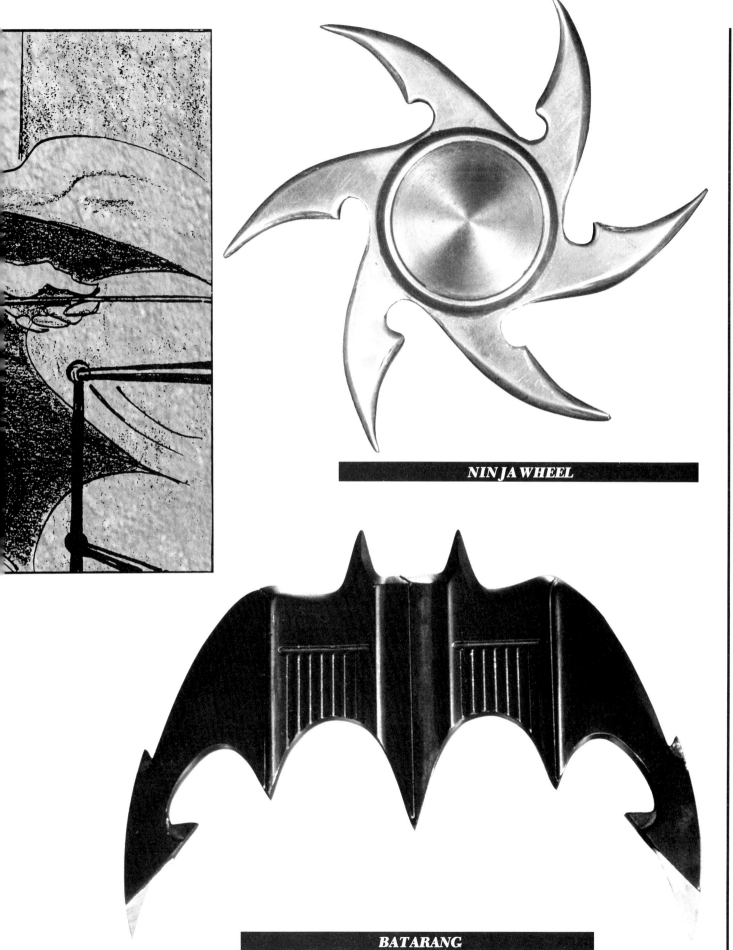

NINJA WHEEL

BATARANG

THE QUILL

THE JOKER'S ARSENAL

Ludicrously long-barrelled gun
Acid flower
Hand-on-a-spring
Telescopic boxing glove
Poison quill pen
High-voltage ring

The Joker's arsenal includes a ludicrously long pistol (which he successfully aims at the Batwing), an acid flower (handy for disfiguring girlfriends and dissolving handcuffs), a hand on a spring (for delivering thoughtful gifts), and a quick-moving boxing-glove, as well as two killer items: a poisoned quill to silence the enemy, and a high voltage ring to fry opponents.

And yet these, though impressive, are no match for Batman's arsenal. At one point, Joker seethes with exasperation: 'Those toys! Where does he get those wonderful toys?' Now we know.

THE ACID FLOWER

THE LONG PISTOL

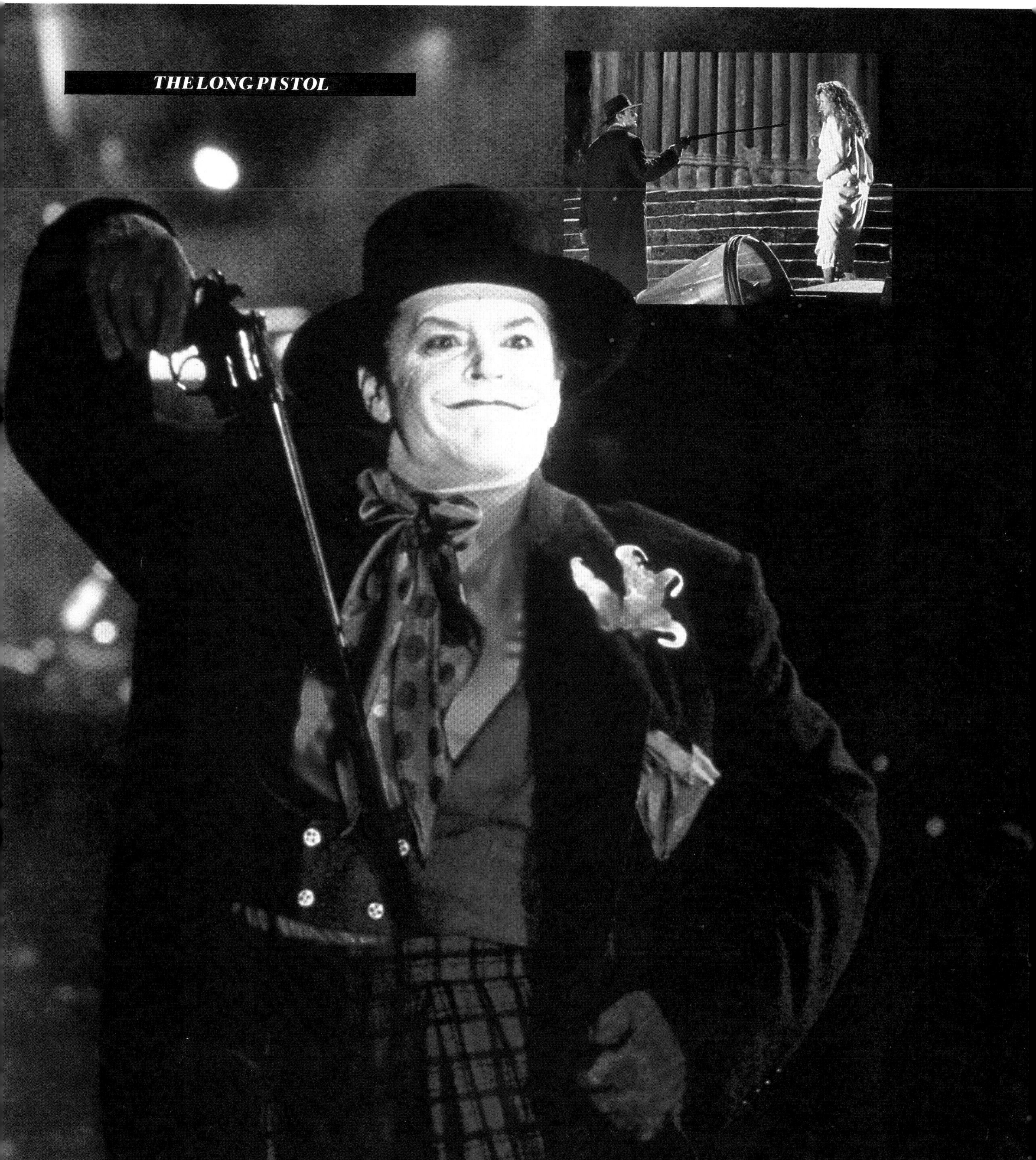

The Joker's willingness to shake hands ought to be a crime in itself. His lethal ring proves handy for frying opponents.

THE STUNTMEN

Stunt co-ordinator Eddie Stacey works closely with John Evans: 'We have a great rapport and have done a lot of pictures together. I design all the stunts, then go to John and ask what kind of effect he can give me.'

Eddie, once a professional boxer and now in the stunt business for 30 years, believes he is 'never too old. I'm 50 years of age but train very hard in my gym at home. You have to be ready to step in.'

Step in he did, when, during The Joker's parade, Eddie steers a car off the street and through a plate glass window. 'This was my first time with plate glass. Normally you use

lose your life, you check everything 100 times. Accidents tend to occur with stunts you take for granted, like falling off a barstool.'

Eddie ensured that Sean McCabe, who is Michael Keaton's stunt double, wore the full safety helmet and firesuit when he drove the Batmobile through flames at the Axis Chemical works. Stacey further explains: 'When working in corridors of fire, an engine can die due to lack of oxygen, so timing is crucial. You see, fire burns up oxygen. Motor-bike riders who weren't aware of this have perished in tunnel-of-fire stunts.'

When it comes to car crashes, Eddie provides safety harnesses, and, when the driver is not in shot, crash helmets too. 'We keep the petrol levels down to a minimum, and have our safety guards, armed with axes, all around the outside, in case anything goes wrong.'

When stuntman Wayne Michaels dangles from the catwalk on a 2 mm wire, with only 40 ft [12m] of nothingness beneath, or when Kim Basinger (and her stunt double, Sy Hollands) shoot through the Flugelheim Museum on equally thin wires, at least they know that endless safety checks have been carried out.

Eddie, who generally picks good all-rounders as stuntmen, lined up Gerry Crampton to double for Jack Nicholson, as well as McCabe for Keaton, and Hollands for Basinger.

'We were very lucky in this film,' Eddie says, 'because Kim, Michael and especially Jack did most of their own work. You must remember that being 50 or 60 ft up in the air on a wire is bad enough for a stuntman, never mind an actor.'

Long shots, when the star is not in close-up, are usually handled by stuntmen. Gerry Crampton falling into the vat of toxic waste is a case in point. However, Crampton, at 59 years old an extremely agile stunt veteran, points to occasions when stars, even if they want to, won't carry out their own stunts: 'Insurance won't cover the stars to do anything too hairy. Take, for example, the sequence at the Flugelheim, which Batman and Vicki bring to a close by smashing through the main doors. Even Jack Nicholson, an extremely gutsy guy, knows when to stop.'

breakaway glass which shatters into small pieces. But plate glass explodes, and could actually have cut through the car like butter.'

In addition to this one-off screen stunt, Eddie personally tested all the wires, as well as the airbags, which are used for soft landings from great heights. Of safety he has the following to say: 'The big stunts are normally very safe, because, since you could

SCARY BUILDINGS AND FUN COSTUMES

Gotham City, 1989, is as menacing as the Joker's grin. More substantial than in the earliest *Detective Comics*, it echoes the cry of despair of a city savaged by juvenile muggers and moneyed killers. The buildings give off a quirky surrealism which is a perfect visual match for not only The Joker, but also Batman himself.

The awesome cityscape, which reeks of a fevered imagination, is the latest creation by production designer Anton Furst. Director Tim Burton describes Furst as 'a kindred spirit and a brilliant production designer'.

According to Anton, he and Tim always wanted the same tonal feel in the film, and believed that Batman's whole world should revert to its sinister origins. The trick was to create a look which was both timeless and yet recognizable to an audience:

'Since no city was ever created by any one designer, we felt it a good idea to go for a pot-pourri of styles which would help us towards a sense of timelessness. The trouble is that, when you're trying hard *not* to resemble a particular look, you're working in a vacuum. The tough part is finding a look which is both different yet believable.'

Right and inset: *Anton Furst's brooding design for Gotham City Hall is nicely balanced by Bob Ringwood's loud suit for The Joker. Both are images of a film which has been propelled by a strong sense of design and colour.*

GOTHAM CITY

The jagged skyline of Gotham City is symbolic of the cut-throat antics of the gangsters in the grim streets below.

ANTON FURST

Special effects whizz-turned-production designer Anton Furst has brought his rich visual instincts from Full Metal Jacket *(1987) and* Company of Wolves *(1984) to this film. Successfully creating an architectural style which is unique yet recognizable, he has mirrored the black world of Gotham City in the stylised savagery of his buildings.*

THE MAIN STREET

The visual centrepiece for much of the action is the city centre which takes in Broad Avenue and Gotham City Square. 'With a main street which is a quarter of a mile long, I am told it's the biggest set since *Cleopatra* (1963). It was certainly a massive challenge to me, since I no longer had the comfort of studios and locations. Without studio rigging to help us work at such high levels, massive cranes were brought into service.' Working flat out with his departmental team of 14 and a construction team of 200, it took only five months to build.

'There were four stages of construction. The buildings are supported by scaffolding and clad in plywood. A plaster, or sometimes fibreglass, covering is added and then finally painted.'

THE MONARCH THEATRE

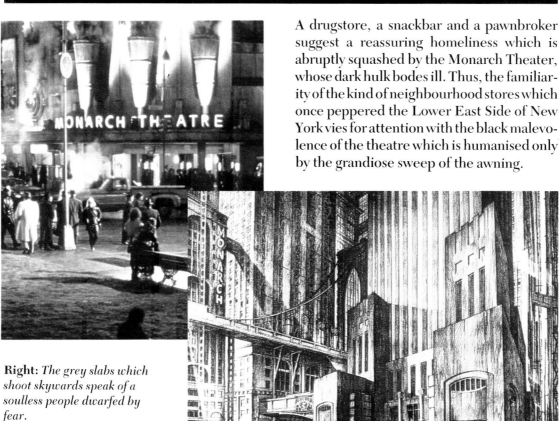

A drugstore, a snackbar and a pawnbroker suggest a reassuring homeliness which is abruptly squashed by the Monarch Theater, whose dark hulk bodes ill. Thus, the familiarity of the kind of neighbourhood stores which once peppered the Lower East Side of New York vies for attention with the black malevolence of the theatre which is humanised only by the grandiose sweep of the awning.

Right: *The grey slabs which shoot skywards speak of a soulless people dwarfed by fear.*

All are dwarfed, however, by the geometric savagery of the Flugelheim Museum whose brutal exterior is more akin to locomotive design than the Guggenheim, whose name it twists amusingly.

Furst regards it as 'one of my most successful designs. I wanted the museum to be a surprise, a new, radical edifice which concealed an older building underneath. The radical broadstroke of the exterior conceals a style which borrows from Otto Wagner as well as brownstone housing.

'The locomotive look of the outside is intentionally balanced by a rooflight on top, through which Batman jumps to save Vicki. Having soft light inside was quite deliberate. I wanted to reverse the notion of a conventional building where you are normally happy to walk back outside into the light. Here, it's just the opposite.'

Above and right: *Locomotive design was a key inspiration for the Flugelheim.*

THE CATHEDRAL

Even the museum, however, is dominated by the Cathedral which is a key dramatic device in the film and which Anton calls 'the establishing part of the city'. 'The problem here was to create a cathedral which was taller than the tallest skyscraper and still make it credible. It had to be over 1,000 feet (300 metres) high. I then remembered that some of the 1930s skyscrapers in New York produced a cathedral effect at the top by means of interesting Gothic detail. I began to solve the puzzle.'

Furst was primarily influenced in his design by Gaudi, the now-feted Spanish architect who is best known for his cone-shaped cathedral in Barcelona. There is no Gothic, Norman, or any other cathedral reference in Gaudi's masterpiece, so its sense of timelessness appealed to Furst and thus fitted the tone of the film.

'I basically stretched Gaudi into a sky-scraper and added a castle feel which was especially influenced by the look of the Japanese fortress.'

The top deck of the Cathedral is strongly evocative of Hitchcock's house, a favourite image, as it happens, of Tim Burton's. The dangerous parapets, as well as the canti-levered belfry, fit the malevolent heart of a city which God left 100 years before. Yet the augmented and exaggerated design, whose unreality still had to be made credible, also suggests the comic absurdity which is evident in the film.

Because filming in and around the Cathedral was very complicated, full-size set-pieces were built on both the lot and the studio to represent the top and bottom of the building, while two other scales were em-ployed to construct the length in between.

AXIS CHEMICAL FACTORY

Away from the city centre, but just as mean-spirited in tone, is the Axis Chemical Works. Resembling a ghastly space-ship which might take off at any moment and destroy the planet, it was once more a result of imaginative planning. 'I didn't want it to look like a shapeless refinery,' claims Furst, 'so I thought I'd make it resemble a huge dam. As you will see, large concrete blocks are locked onto turn-of-the-century architecture, so we've achieved another interesting contrast there.'

The massive bulk of the building is offset by a high window which is used in the movie to reflect The Joker's manic grin. It is The Joker's loud suits which Furst uses to help

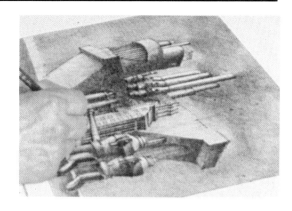

orchestrate the drama of colour. 'The effect here really works. Whenever you see him, his appearance shouts at you from a background of subdued tones.'

INTERIORS

Colourful too, a soft, creamy beige in fact, is Vicki Vale's apartment. A deliberate contrast to the monumental threat of the other buildings, its interior befits the persona of a career girl on the make. Inspired primarily by the Scot, Charles Rennie Mackintosh, the apartment is dominated by curves, which suggest Vicki's femininity and sensuality. Even the walls are rounded. However, both to avoid the home-of-a-film-star look and also to suggest her independence, the decor was picked out in black.

Top: *Anton Furst working on production drawings for the Axis Chemical Factory.*

Above left: *As evidenced by the god-like heads outside his apartment, Carl Grissom is chief gangster bar none. Classical-style columns, a mogul-size desk and a handy globe all suggest a monster ego with little patience for opposition.*

Left: *A world away from the ugly exteriors which loom over Gotham City is the soft interior of Vicki's apartment, where colours and curves suggest both her goodness and femininity.*

At first, the muscles on Batman's suit moved in a different direction from Michael Keaton's own muscles. Four prototypes were made before both sets moved in tandem.

Having emerged from the Batwing with only superficial injuries Batman stares through a headpiece which looks like a further layer of his own skin.

BATMAN'S COSTUME

The body of Batman's costume was made of lycra, a material familiar to those who wear dance costumes. A foam rubber cast was then glued on top.

'It was at first difficult for Michael Keaton to move convincingly,' recalls Bob. 'For example, the muscles on the suit moved in a different direction from Michael's own muscles. We actually made four prototypes before we got it right. The result is a very light outfit, though you might find Michael disagreeing!'

Although the cape itself is quite heavy, the whole is nothing as compared with the 400lb (180kg) outfits which actors are often forced to wear on television costume dramas.

Batman's helmet-style headpiece also caused Bob moments of anxiety: 'We had to fit the seams in such a way that they didn't show on camera. Since the outfit has to look as though it's part of his body, the magical impact would be lost forever if you could see the seams.'

Relaxed millionaire Bruce Wayne is at all times casually smart, dressed as he is in modern clothes, albeit with a slight Forties flair.

BOB RINGWOOD

Could reading 400 comics knock you sideways for life? Costume designer Bob Ringwood wouldn't say, but admitted he did just that by way of research. As a youngster, he had never read the Batman comics and, when designing the outfits, he consciously avoided the TV series whose tone is at odds with the film. Bob secured his contract in much the same manner as did Jerry Hall. Unable to join the Bond film, *Licence to Kill* (1989), in Mexico, he was at Pinewood Studios when he ran into co-producer, Chris Kenny. He met Tim Burton for ten minutes, and the result is a splash of eccentric designs.

ALICIA AND THE GOONS

Suggestive too of the Forties era are the suits and dresses of Alicia, favourite lady of both Carl Grissom and Jack Napier. Jerry Hall, 'a very nice, very funny lady', according to Bob, was very helpful. 'I went to her house, she went through her wardrobe and paraded her clothes for me.'

She looks a lot more glamorous than either the Goons, whose leather-jacket look was inspired by New York's Guardian Angels or Jack Palance, whose gangster outfit was one of 200 unused Forties suits found in a New York warehouse.

THE JOKER'S SUITS

Facing the same problem as Anton Furst of creating costumes which were unique, yet believable, he hit on what he calls 'a soft sell retro Forties' or 'timeless modern' look.

The Joker appears in what are in essence Forties-style, double-breasted three-piece suits. It was, says Bob, quite customary to wear a waistcoat with this kind of suit at that time. Yet no Forties suit would have sported the dayglo colours favoured by The Joker. Preferring dark blue and mulberry attire as the vain Jack Napier, he soon learns to blind the city as The Joker, whose increasing psychosis is reflected in his noisy dress. Tailored blues soon make way for purple, red and green, colours which are also a by-product of his toxic accident.

Purple too, is his hat, which, as Ringwood points out, is really a pork-pie classic, while the gaudy colours of his tail-coat decorate the standard conservative model.

All the clothes were designed with Nicholson's stocky frame in mind and Ringwood is pleased to say that 'Jack was really happy to go along with my ideas. He really loves clothes anyway and is very easy to dress.' Like others, Ringwood reinforces the view that Nicholson, with his reportedly excessive lifestyle, is tailor-made for the role.

Wardrobe assistant Dave Whiting had special responsibility for dressing Jack Nicholson. He believes that: 'Young people will latch onto a lot of the fashions which will come out of this movie.' The high streets of the world could soon look very different.

Below: *The heavy browns of Grissom and his hoods will soon be replaced.*

Above: *The florid purple of The Joker, who goes on to restyle his pack of Goons.*

'I'm the world's first fully-functioning homicidal artist! And I want my face on the one dollar bill.'

BATMAN

CREW LIST

Director	Tim Burton
Producers	Jon Peters
	Peter Guber
Co-Producer	Chris Kenny
Executive Producers	Benjamin Melniker
	Michael Uslan
Screenwriters	Sam Hamm
	Warren Skaaren
Assistant Director	Derek Cracknell
Supervising Production Accountant	Mike Smith
Production Designer	Anton Furst
Supervising Art Director	Les Tomkins
Art Directors	Terry Ackland-Snow
	Nigel Phelps
Set Decorator	Peter Young
Storyboard Artist	Michael White
Property Master	Charles Torbett
Casting Director	Marion Dougherty
Director of Photography	Roger Pratt
Camera Operators	Mike Proudfoot
	John Campbell
Script Supervisor	Cheryl Leigh
Chief Electrician	Chuck Finch
Sound Mixer	Tony Dawe
Film Editor	Ray Lovejoy
Supervising Sound Editor	Don Sharpe
Costume Designer	Bob Ringwood
Chief Make-Up Artist	Paul Engelen
Prosthetic Chief Make-Up Artist	Nick Dudman
Chief Hairdresser	Colin Jamison
Visual Effects Supervisor	Derek Meddings
Director of Photography (Miniatures)	Paul Wilson
Special Effects Supervisor	John Evans
Construction Manager	Terry Apsey

SECOND UNIT

Director/Cameraman	Peter Macdonald
Assistant Director	Steven Harding
Camera Operator	Mike Brewster
Sound	David Allen
Chief Electrician	Bob Bremner

CAST LIST

Jack Napier/The Joker	Jack Nicholson
Bruce Wayne/Batman	Michael Keaton
Vicki Vale	Kim Basinger
Carl Grissom	Jack Palance
Alexander Knox	Robert Wuhl
Harvey Dent	Billy Dee Williams
Commissioner Gordon	Pat Hingle
Alicia	Jerry Hall
Alfred	Michael Gough
Mayor Borg	Lee Wallace
Bob the Goon	Tracey Walter
Eckhardt	Williams Hootkins
Rotelli	Edwin Craig
Ricorso	John Dair
Doctor	Steve Plytas
Goon	Richard Strange
Goon	Carl Chase
Goon	Mac MacDonald
Goon	George Cooper
Goon	Phil Tan
Goon	Terence Plummer
Young Jack Napier	Hugo E Blick
Young Bruce Wayne	Charles Roskilly
Eddie	George Roth
Nick	Christopher Fairbank
Mr Wayne	David Baxt
Mrs Wayne	Sharon Holm